EMPIRE OF DETERRENCE

EMPIRE OF DETERRENCE

NUCLEAR WEAPONS & THE CONTAINMENT OF POLITICS

Michael Gardiner

01 14
√ √

Published by Repeater Books

An imprint of Watkins Media Ltd

Unit 11 Shepperton House

89-93 Shepperton Road

London

N1 3DF

United Kingdom

www.repeaterbooks.com

A Repeater Books paperback original 2025

1

Distributed in the United States by Random House, Inc., New York.

ISBN: 9781917516037

Ebook ISBN: 9781917516044

The manufacturer's authorised representative in the EU for product safety is: eucomply OÜ - Pärnu mnt 139b-14, 11317 Tallinn, Estonia, hello@eucompliancepartner.com, www.eucompliancepartner.com

Printed and bound by CPI Group (UK) Ltd, Croydon, CR0 4YY

CONTENTS

NUKES
AND ENLIGHTENMENT

It is possible to identify three broad eras of nuclear pressure. The first ran roughly from the late 1950s to the early '60s, and saw the establishment of an 'overkill' level of thermonuclear force, the open-ended adoption of Mutually Assured Destruction (with all its moments of nervous emergency), and an agreement on the part of superpowers and declining powers about the moral need to put humanity on the line. The second era ran from the late 1970s to the late '80s — through Soviet movements in Europe and Atlantic neoliberal governments' escalation against the communist threat — and gave us much of the imagery that still stands for nuclear threat. The third, beginning somewhere around the start of the 2010s, has been characterised, on the contrary, by a relative lack of cultural imagination and a struggle to have nuclear readiness recognised as a political question at all. The emergencies of the first two nuclear eras still provide most of the cultural shorthands for nuclear threat, often now presented in a retro or quirky form — though many metrics put the danger higher in the 2020s than during the Cold War. Nuclear threat, as we're aware without often saying so, never disappeared, it just became difficult to think. In part this depoliticisation results from pressures that were enabled precisely by the victory in the Cold War, particularly the war on attention fought by American tech. Post-Cold War globalisation helped get nuclear weapons pushed under the threshold at which they could be seen as political, with the political redefined in terms of more visible issues with more immediate payoffs.

The nuclear imagination struggles, that is, under the regime of weaponised distraction enabled by the American Cold War victory itself. Attention to nuclear violence has been almost entirely replaced by attention to violence against the typologies laid out for individuals, or violence against identities. Identities are tradeable qualities. Identities yield value, and so does the defence of identities. It's not that the defence of the individual value yielded by identities is not political compared to nuclear politics, but that this defence is not really political at all — it is post-political; it has replaced politics as shared historical struggle. The post-political is what the superweapon will always try to guide us back towards. When the scope of the political is progressively reduced like this, the abstracted, mass violence of nukes, and their ability to carve up space and disable populations, becomes more difficult to see. For Benoît Pelopidas, the ability to imagine nuclear war is crucial to being able to see nuclear disarmament as even a general possibility: without cultures depicting nuclear violence, or cultures depicting a world after nuclear weapons, the extinction unconscious settles into place unopposed.[1] In what follows, I take up this reminder of the need to pick out the stakes of nuclear violence amid a stream of information with more obvious immediate cultural capital, and ask how Cold War cultures might

---

1   Benoît Pelopidas, 'Imaginer la possibilité de la guerre nucléaire pour y faire face', *Cultures & Conflits* 123–4, Autumn-Winter 2021, 173–212.

be reconsidered as resources against the identity-extinction complex.

Nuclear realism needs permanent crisis. Only within permanent crisis can the continuity of nukes be assumed. Nowhere is this more obvious than in the UK, the first leader of both nuclear technology and nuclear moralism, and the main focus of this book. In this nuclear weapons state, no political party larger than the SNP has touched the subject of nuclear disarmament since the 1980s. Since their adoption, and even before, nukes have been deemed normal and natural. The nuclear superweapon, the weapon able to command all space, is homely in Britain in a particularly intractable way. When Elaine Scarry considers the capture of sovereignty by 'out-of-ratio' weapons — weapons that constitute a general existential threat but which are controlled by tiny groups — she goes back to the founding conditions of British citizenship. Out-of-ratio weapons mark a democratic foreclosure, a point at which the protection of official democracy begins to make actual democracy impossible, and meaningful progress ends.[2]

The out-of-ratio weapon, for Scarry, turns societies that start as democracies into 'thermonuclear monarchies'. Scarry contrasts the thermonuclear monarchy with the social contract associated with the foundational promise made in John Locke's *Second Treatise on Government*, and points towards a revivification of that document's sentiment. However, what characterises Locke's citizens is that they only become citizens through property, through a command of the stuff of the world, reducing it to what can be evaluated, utilised, and exchanged. The progress described by Locke's *Second Treatise* is indexed to the ability to keep extending stable evaluation across the world, or the

---

2   Elaine Scarry, *Thermonuclear Monarchy: Choosing Between Democracy and Doom* (New York: Norton, 2014), 25.

ability to command space and exert Enlightment over all places instantly. So Lockean government has the rationale of the nuclear superweapon; or, the nuclear superweapon follows the naturalised version of sovereignty that follows the Lockean revolution at the end of the seventeenth century. The Lockean social contract, moreover, promises that the universal market will gradually eliminate physical conflict. Such a Newtonianism of government reduces social belonging to a universal arithmetic, and its concept of progress lies in vanquishing all conflict that can't be abstracted for financial arbitration.[3]

By the time of the Scottish Enlightenment, this spread of Newtonian laws would frequently be understood as corresponding to universal laws of progress. For Adam Smith and many others, a singular historical path to civilisation, passing through stages of respect for property, could be discovered empirically and was expected to hold across all societies and all times. Tellingly, this commitment to a singular history became particularly pronounced from the mid-1740s — the point at which the last of the highland rebellions were killed off and abstracted market rationality would spread unimpeded across the whole new Britain. The 1746 Disarming Act banned barbaric weapons and effectively demanded that conflict be sublimated to the universal arithmetic — a path that would lead progressively to the superweapon. The superweapon amplifies this promise to overcome the barbarism of physical violence, replacing embodied conflict with identity competition, abstracting its own harm right up to the point where it becomes unthinkable.

---

3   John Locke, ed. Peter Laslett, *Two Treatises of Government* (Cambridge: Cambridge University Press, 1988 (1689)); A. Richard Hall, *All Was Light: An Introduction to Newton's* Opticks (Oxford: Clarendon, 2019), 45.

Moreover, as all space was progressively evened out to take away local conflicts and replace them with universal evaluation, representation also had to become progressively clearer. Representation, for writers of the Scottish Enlightenment, tends towards transparency in mature commercial societies, and to reveal the world as a collection of objects for exchange. This is the drive to clarity that characterises the Anglosphere, but it also characterises nuclear threat, which requires that all parties have an equal understanding of each gambit being made. Nuclear threat is ultimately, as Jean Baudrillard and others would describe it, an exchange of fictional proposals: a rhetorical competition. But although the delicate balance of terror requires a transparent language, nukes' reliance on transparent language is also their fatal flaw. Clear communication has to be assumed, but statements from outwith the Anglosphere commercial empire come to seem opaque and threatening — for instance, the paranoid speculation over the Soviets' intentions that marked some of the worst brushes with apocalypse of the second nuclear era. Some awareness of this fatal opacity is fairly common in second-nuclear-era culture. Troy Kennedy Martin's nuclear *noir* TV series *Edge of Darkness* (1985), for example, in which plutonium entrepreneurialism in deregulated markets, seen as having the potential to spread enlightenment across the galaxy, depends on an underground knowledge — the plutonium is only made visible by a local miner's tunnelling to an underground bunker (months after the miners' strike).[4] In *Edge of Darkness* the plutonium brings an invisible sickness that tracks the narrative from the metropolis to the stormy Scottish mountains and the fading of the anti-hero. The promise of clear space always conceals a shadowy under-

---

4   Wr. Troy Kennedy Martin, dir. Martin Campbell, *Edge of Darkness*, BBC, 1985.

side like this; Anglosphere civilization is eternal, but it is accompanied by an extinction unconscious.

Nukes, then, the violent form of the drive to clear space and universal evaluation, always carry something of the Atlantic Enlightenment in them. The point is not that the Anglosphere is the world's only nuclear threat, or its greatest nuclear threat, or that Anglosphere disarmament would solve the problem of despotic nuclear blackmail elsewhere in the world. It's that the naturalisation of nukes has the Atlantic demand for spatial control written into it even when it passes into non-Atlantic hands; it is the characteristic type of conflict of a now-passing era of Atlantic hegemony.

The drive to the superweapon, moreover, became urgent when the Anglosphere seemed to come under threat, around the end of the nineteenth century, with the British empire contracting and American fears of invasion rising. The old Lockean-Smithian powers would frequently be realigned in what was known, in England at least, as a 'Greater Britain'. Greater Britain was a political, cultural, and linguistic alliance of those parts of the world characterised by Anglosphere progressiveness. Particularly in the context of a drastic modernisation of weaponry (since the 1870–71 Franco-Prussian War in particular), it was conceived as a defensive union. Greater Britain had to be vigilant against illiberal Europeans, rising colonials, and fifth columns of Irish socialists, and develop its defences against barbaric forces. By World War One — the obvious starting point of massified weapons — European weapons had expanded almost beyond recognition, as had the willingness to attack populations, or to see populations as comprising combatants. Speculation about superweapons proliferate in the press and in popular fiction between the 1910s and '30s, and featured matter-changing forces, bioweapons, death rays, and most often, poison gas, a field heavily supported by the British establishment. Atomic research fit neatly into this superweapon imagination, and it largely originated in England — most prominently, the 1900s–10s work of Ernest Rutherford and Frederick Soddy, which demonstrated radioactive decay and created the first artificial nuclear reaction.

Correspondingly, early nuclear weapons cultures were also overwhelmingly based in the Anglosphere. The first apocalyptic story of radioactive weapons was probably Roy Norton's *The Vanishing Fleets* (1907), which described the use of matter-displacing 'radioplanes'.[5] The marker for most cultural histories, though, is H.G. Wells's far-seeing story of nuclear apocalypse — and conscious transmission of Rutherford and Soddy — *The World Set Free* (1914–15).[6] *The World Set Free* is a strange celebration of Anglosphere technocracy, a nuclear dystopia that gives way to a liberal utopia. In a drastic acceleration of Locke's reformism, here Wells has empiricist science *itself* proclaimed king — though not before the superweapon has seen to the world's cities. Although the new atomic energy technology has the potential to 'make the whole world one smiling Garden of Eden', as a weapon it attracts oligarchs and is 'only awaiting a suitable detonator to cause the earth to revert to chaos'.[7] This it does, in devastating atomic blasts in which 'flying fragments clamber up towards the zenith. Against the glare I saw the country-side for miles standing black and clear, churches, trees, chimneys'.[8] Wells even tracks this passage to atomic war through the Scottish Enlightenment's universal history — a civilisational ascent through agricultural

---

5   Roy Norton, *The Vanishing Fleets* (New York: D. Appleton, 1908).

6   H.G. Wells, *The World Set Free* (New York: E.P. Dutton, 1914).

7   Wells, *The World Set Free*, 25, 32–33.

8   Wells, *The World Set Free*, 139.

surplus, then the power of steam, to 'the snare that will some day catch the sun'.[9] But human psychology lags behind, struggling to adapt old barbaric tendencies quickly enough, and nations descend into 'a delirium of panic, in order to use their bombs first'.[10] However, populations are held together by a liberal empiricism that helps them through the post-apocalyptic world, shaking them 'out of their old established habits of thought, and out of the lightly held beliefs and prejudices that came down to them from the past', and eventually teaching them to live with perpetual deterrence under a post-political, English-speaking world.[11] Apocalypse is a bump on the road to a benevolent world technocracy like the technocracy wished for in Wells's influential *Open Conspiracy* (1928), for which empiricism should be recognised as a world religion.

If Wells's strange empiricist utopia says a lot about the foundations of Atlantic nuclear realism, nevertheless it would be countered by a familiar line of dystopias leading all the way to George Orwell's *Nineteen Eighty-Four* (1949). Orwell's best-known novel is rarely remembered as the post-nuclear-war story. But more than this, as Raymond Williams would note, in Orwell the expansion of government surveillance is fundamentally dependent on atomic command.[12] Behind *Nineteen Eighty-Four*'s liberalism gone bad is a superweapon carefully distinguished from the conventional bombs that still stood for British cohesion: Winston's earliest memory is of going 'down, down, down' into a tube station to shelter, as if in the Blitz. But when he

---

9   Wells, *The World Set Free*, 15.

10   Wells, *The World Set Free*, 152.

11   Wells, *The World Set Free*, 254.

12   Raymond Williams, 'The Politics of Nuclear Disarmament', in ed. E.P. Thompson, *Exterminism and Cold War* (London: New Left Review, 1982 (1980)) 65–85: 70–71.

emerges, he finds there is no world to rebuild. In fact, Orwell likely had the coming atomic war in mind throughout the writing of his book, moving to the Scottish island of Jura and reasoning that 'the only hope is to have a home with a few animals in some place not worth a bomb'.[13] 'Orwellian' government is nuclear government. Oceania is Greater Britain after nukes — its name even revisits J.A. Froude's classic *Oceana* (1886), a Greater Britain travelogue that celebrates the shared cultural and commercial aims of English-speaking peoples. In the post-nuclear Greater Britain, the defence emergency has become permanent; natural law has become an inescpable historicism; laws have become instincts that precede all political thought; and continental-style police show the real violence behind the British iconography of cabbage-smelling corridors and cosy consensus.

Orwell had already described the social and political demands of a permanent superweapon standoff in his October 1945 *Tribune* essay 'You and the Atom Bomb'.[14] The complexity of producing the weapon, Orwell argues, drastically reduced the number of people with any physical stake in conflict, and the concentration of the means of war threatened to make populations expendable. The A-Bomb's eclipse of citizens follows from Locke's reduction of citizens to market actors; but as Orwell prefigures Scarry in describing, this already brings a form of tyranny:

> Ages in which the dominant weapon is expensive or difficult to make will tend to be ages of despotism, whereas when

13   Stephen Metcalf, 'What Orwell Really Feared', *The Atlantic*, 5 April 2024: theatlantic.com/magazine/archive/2024/05/george-orwell-1984-isle-of-jura/677843/

14   George Orwell, 'You and the Atom Bomb', *Tribune,* 19 October 1945: orwell.ru/library/articles/ABomb/english/e_abomb

the dominant weapon is cheap and simple, the common people have a chance. Thus, for example, tanks, battleships and bombing planes are inherently tyrannical weapons, while rifles, muskets, long-bows and hand-grenades are inherently democratic weapons.

Nukes complete this great exclusion. Or as Scarry says, they 'delete populations'. They make peoples dependent on

two or three monstrous super-states, each possessed of a weapon by which millions of people can be wiped out in a few seconds, dividing the world between them. It has been rather hastily assumed that this means bigger and bloodier wars, and perhaps an actual end to the machine civilisation. But suppose — and really this the likeliest development — that the surviving great nations make a tacit agreement never to use the atomic bomb against one another? Suppose they only use it, or the threat of it, against people who are unable to retaliate? In that case we are back where we were before, the only difference being that power is concentrated in still fewer hands and that the outlook for subject peoples and oppressed classes is still more hopeless.[15]

This would remain the default form of nuclear sovereignty — a general condition of 'robbing the exploited classes and peoples of all power to revolt', and marked by the ascendancy of a form of government 'at once unconquerable and in a permanent state of "cold war" with its neighbours'.[16] This is the world of tyranny Williams would describe as fitting nuclear realism; later it would be the world described by Antonio Negri and Félix Guattari as under nuclear threat

---

15   Orwell, 'You and the Atom Bomb'.
16   Famously, this may have been the first use of the term Cold War.

leveraged by 'Integrated World Capital'.[17] Although nuclear threat would come to be used by powers far beyond the Atlantic, the kind of empire-building it implies is not so much that of the old military conquest as it is the worlding proper to the Atlantic Enlightenment.

Despite counter-Wellsian scepticism, the liberal vision of the early Wells would directly influence material advances in nuclear weapons. Nukes were imagined, then they were built. Leo Szilard, pioneer of the fission chain reaction, describes how when he created the first nuclear pile (an early reactor made of layers of fissile material), 'all the things which H.G. Wells predicted appeared suddenly real to me'.[18] The Manhattan Project would take Wells as its unofficial godfather.[19] By this point the need to protect singular development was beginning to make the space-unifying weapon seem inevitable. In March 1940, the Frisch-Peierls Memorandum, originating in the University of Birmingham, outlined the mechanism of a U235 bomb; later that year the MAUD Committee, convened to digest scientific research across English universities, concluded not only that an atomic weapon was feasible, but also that it should be used irrespective of whether it provided any real gain in the war.[20]

---

17   Antonio Negri and Félix Guattari, *Communists Like Us* (New York: Semiotext(e), 1995 (1985)).

18   Eds. Spencer R. Weart and Getrud Weiss Szilard, *Leo Szilard: His Version of the Facts*, Vol.2 (Cambridge, MA: MIT Press, 1978), 17, 57; Richard Rhodes, *The Making of the Atomic Bomb* (London: Simon and Schuster, 2012 (1986)), 24.

19   David Seed, *Under the Shadow: The Atomic Bomb and Cold War Narratives* (Kent, OH: Kent State University Press, 2013), 17, 19; David Edgerton, *England and the Aeroplane: Militarism, Modernity and Machines* (London: Penguin, 2013), 17.

20   Roger Ruston, *A Say in the End of the World: Morals and*

This determination to establish nuclear supremacy, and the Orwellian secrecy it demands, marks a final developmental stage of an Enlightenment that has been left to fossilise. Liberal promises of prosperity and freedom seem at this point to have been exhausted, and violence turns inwards towards populations. This nuclear hardening can be seen as a kind of market destiny: the future is formally open — free property, free choice, freedom from kings — but at the same time, an irreversible hardwiring of Mutually Assured Destruction means that the future is already over. In Francis Fukuyama's post–Cold War book *The End of History and the Last Man* — which popularised the idea of an end of history (its title echoing Orwell's draft title, *The Last Man in Europe*) — the destination of liberalism is the permanent destruction of political barbarism, just as it had been for eighteenth century liberals. The old historicism specifically aims to neutralise the Soviets' 'updated Marxism that threatened to lead to the ultimate apocalypse of nuclear war'.[21] In terms of nuclear stability, Fukuyama's triumphal end of history would only last about a decade before rearmament and geopolitical rivalries again became too obvious to deny. But what nukes' end of history means more widely is the permanent overcoming of physical conflict, a 'disarming' of populations that goes on eternally and is imagined to contain no barbarism itself.

Something like this shadowy recursion of barbarism may be familiar from Theodor Adorno and Max Horkheimer's *Dialectic of Enlightenment* (1947). Placing the terminus of

British Nuclear Weapons Policy 1941–1987 (Oxford: Oxford University Press, 2002 (1989)) 36.

21   Francis Fukuyama, 'The End of History?', *The National Interest* 16, Summer 1989, 3–18; Liam Sprod, *Nuclear Futurism: The Work of Art in the Age of Remainderless Destruction* (Winchester: Zer0, 2012), 4.

the Enlightenment's singular progress in the Nazi regime, *Dialectic of Enlightenment* was drafted just before the demonstration of the first atomic bombs, but only published just after. It describes an abstract rationality that reduces everything it touches to evaluation, strips away pre-existing characteristics in a 'dissolvent rationality', and reduces language to calculation, the perfectly clear, unmetaphorical representation of exchange willed by Scottish Enlightenment writers (and the real basis of the statement that in this modernity there could be 'no poetry').[22] Enlightenment's promise to wipe away myth and darkness conceals a deeper barbarism that typically goes undeclared, then appears as nightmare.[23] When Enlightenment historicism loses its moral impetus, it tends towards a form of automation, and '[t]hinking objectifies itself, and becomes an impersonation of the machine... so that ultimately the machine can replace it'.[24] This automation is that of a fixed history and of nuclear systems, and it appears in the culture industries Adorno and Horkheimer suspect so deeply, particularly the light-unifying technology of the screen, as '[r]eal life is becoming indistinguishable from the movies'.[25] Something similar would be sensed by the later Wells, who, between the writing and publishing of *Dialectic of Enlightenment*, faced with the real atomic bomb, came to see progress as infused with a new emptiness, and citizens as resembling actors in a film.[26] Behind the unification of space in Hollywood film stands the unification of space as

---

22   Adorno and Horkheimer, *Dialectic of Enlightenment* (London: Verso, 2016 (1947)), 3–7, 10–13, 18–19, 37.

23   Adorno and Horkheimer, *Dialectic of Enlightenment*, 3.

24   Adorno and Horkheimer, *Dialectic of Enlightenment*, 25.

25   Adorno and Horkheimer, *Dialectic of Enlightenment*, 126.

26   H.G. Wells, *Mind at the End of its Tether* (London: Heinemann, 1945).

an even abstraction of violence, the space of universal evaluation. Nukes rise to protect this arrangement of space, pulling individuals away from their embodied social place and towards their duties of evaluation and consumption. The nuclear condition, like the condition of the citizen-actor in the troubled later Wells, always involves some degree of cognitive dissonance. Or rather, cognitive dissonance marks the widespread acceptance of extinction-range weapons in otherwise democratic and even socialist societies. Perhaps nowhere is this cognitive dissonance as visible as in the British welfare state after 1945, an official empowering of the masses with world-ending weapons as its anchor.

NUKES VERSUS PLACE

The world-commanding superweapon that came into being in the Atlantic in the early twentieth century was technologically specific, but it was also a product of a much longer civilizational mission. At the heart of this civilizational mission was an expectation of the standardisation of space. The superweapon is the weapon that can eviscerate all places instantly, subjecting all places to strategic command and forcing them to modify for the imperative of evaluation. Theoretically, nukes could have been invented by any world power; in practice, they built on an imperative to control space that was specific to Atlantic empire and its expectation that places will yield up resources and produce empirically verifiable progress. Space-unifying weapons emerge as part of a flattening of the world, a desire to make all places equivalent and interchangeable. Superweapons are fundamental to the mature regime of extraction, not just because they threaten violence, but more fundamentally because the promise to eviscerate all places maintains the spatial unification in which value can be produced (and progress activated, and so on). Even after decades of highly technological wars, it was the nuclear-weapons breakthrough in the mid-twentieth century that signalled the opportunity for the Atlantic empire to become fully global.

In the nuclear era, correspondingly, threats have always seemed to come from beyond this unified space. Although there's some logic to the claim that the immediate justification for the 1945 atomic bombings of Hiroshima and

Nagasaki was to prevent any more American casualties, beyond this was a much longer rationale that had little to do with the war. The British MAUD Report, co-ordinating the creation of the new weapon, insisted that it should be used irrespective of events, something corroborated by a 1945 US Interim Committee which recommended bombing even if it was not needed.[1] Japan, in fact, had long been imaged as an ideal target for the superweapon, since it seemed to constitute a powerful outside to the spatial unification holding together Atlantic commercial empire; Japan signalled an excess of place.

In fact Japan had long been imagined as a target in American science fiction speculating about the coming superweapons. By the time of the atomic bombings, Japan had long since overtaken the Chinese as the main threat in the old motif of the 'yellow peril'. Calls for a pre-emptive bombing of Japan had risen gradually since the Russo-Japanese War (1904–05), to become common by the mid-1930s, with the iconic bomber-hero Billy Mitchell, for example, advocating for the destruction of Japanese cities.[2] In 1941 the science-fiction writer Robert Heinlein imagined American scientists developing 'A-bomb rockets' that could be targeted according to race and would be set to destroy Asians.[3] In the same year, Heinlein's 'Solution Unsatisfactory' had the developers of an atomic bomb enthuse that 'we can declare a Pax Americana and enforce

---

1   William Walker, *A Perpetual Menace: Nuclear Weapons and the International Order* (Abingdon: Routledge, 2012), 32; Ruston, *A Say in the End of the World*, 86.

2   H. Bruce Franklin, *War Stars: The Superweapon and The American Imagination* (New York: Oxford University Press, 1988), 97–100.

3   Robert Heinlein, *Sixth Column* (Riverdale, NY: Baen, 2012 (1941)).

it'.[4] Hastily inaugurated in 1945, President Truman had himself grown up with the superweapon science fiction that filled magazines like *Astounding* and often described why the atomic weapon would be necessary.[5] A flow of 'new yellow peril' propaganda was joined by the internment of around twelve thousand part-Japanese residents. Though the nuclear hegemon was, by the time of the millennium, maintaining its moral high ground largely through nagging on 'race', it had this racialisation at its origin. In turn, the '45 bombings would be seen by many American strategists as a platform for extending reach over Asia, and atomic bombings would be considered for use in proxy wars, including Korea — notably by Douglas MacArthur, who had been supreme commander for the Allied Powers during the Japanese occupation (1945–48).

But more fundamentally, what made the Japanese Empire ripe for nuclear disciplining was its commitment to un-abstracted, embodied conflict. Japanese history was not committed enough to the deathless continuity that characterised world commercial empire. The country's 'modernising' period, the Meiji era (1868–1912), had ended with a wave of ritual suicides following Emperor Meiji's death; by the end of World War Two, the spectre of *tokkeitai* (suicide bombers) haunted figures at the top of the Anglo-American establishment in the Second World War, including Winston Churchill, who saw this tendency to put one's body on the line as a clear mark of barbarism. The Meiji era had even opened, like the period that 'cultured' British union and saw British commercial empire rise over localised vi-

---

4   Robert Heinlein (as Anson MacDonald), 'Solution Unsatisfactory', *Astounding* 27–3 (1941): https://archive.org/details/ Astounding_v27n03_1941-05/page/n55/mode/2up?view=theater.
5   Franklin, *War Stars*, 42; Ruston, *A Say in the End of the World*, 85, 86.

olence, with Japan's own 'Disarming Act' (1876), which saw sword-wearing proscribed in an uncanny echo of the 1746 proscription visited on Scottish Jacobites. Progress depended on the abstraction of conflict; failures of abstraction resulted in a country's ejection from the liberal world order and made them a legitimate target.

Japan's emergence as a modern state had itself depended on an adaptation to the Atlantic Enlightenment world. The country's first ruling elite had been armed and educated by British opium traders carrying Smithian ideas of marketisation east from China; the Scottish Enlightenment insistence that progress depended on the rise of property through predictable stages to that of commercial society had been channeled faithfully into the 'Meiji Enlightenment' of the 1870s. The Meiji state, like the early British state, itself stood for a move into the light (*mei* is light; *ji* is government) — this form of modernity, tracking British development, was a move towards uniform space. At the other end of Meiji, the expectation of unified space had begun to hit trouble, and with it the absolutely evaluable world, and the form of progress that saw the rise of the evaluating individual as inevitable. The country that threatens to interrupt unified space becomes an enemy of modernity. Something like this can be seen in the cultural field of light critiques that abounded in the 1920s and '30s — responses to the commercialisation of Tokyo in particular. In Tanizaki Jun'ichirō's *In'ei Raisan/In Praise of Shadows* (1933), a light-flooded Tokyo shows how each place in the world will be turned into commodities arranged around consumer-citizens. Tanizaki imagines a domestic interior that will offer a place free from the illumination that makes everything knowable and objective, a place where there are still spots of belonging marked by shadowiness or cloudiness — lacquer bowls, jade, *shoji* (sliding paper doors). This cloudiness is a kind of haunting, suggesting memories that have not been eviscerated by the singular progressive history — the persistence of place, or what Mark Fisher called the 'staining' of a place. Tanizaki, though, fears the coming of an even greater disciplining light as global commercial empire extends its authority, bringing more places into the spatial unity. What he foresees looks uncannily like a nuclear blast — it eviscerates the senses, burns away the body, and destroys shadowy spots of belonging.[6] What it leaves is pure continuity, or as François Bonnet has described, eternity as a perpetual present without shadows.[7]

The rejection of Atlantic universalism, then, can't be reduced to the discontent of military imperialists, even if later American accounts typically described it as such. This was a primary aim of Kyoto School philosophy, a broad tradition arising from a desire to rethink world history as Euro-American world history. Following Nishida Kitarō to the ancient capital and adopting his project of reworking Euro-American thought, Kyoto tackled the attractions of a singular progress lingering throughout Euro-American philosophical tradition, but they also set themselves against the domestic militarism and ultranationalism that reached its pinnacle of authority with the 1941 takeover by Tōjō Hideki. And yet, at least until around the turn of the millennium, Kyoto philosophy tended to be written off as complicit with Japanese war atrocities. In fact, this tendency is seen in as unlikely a figure as Slavoj Žižek, who rejects what he sees as a Buddhist complicity with war crimes, as if they are some kind of fate to be accepted with a Zen shrug.[8] This probably says more about Žižek's assumptions

---

6   Tanizaki Jun'ichirō, *In'ei Raisan* (Tokyo: Chūkō, 2009 (1933)), 59.

7   François J. Bonnet, *After Death* (Falmouth: Urbanomic, 2021 (2019)).

8   Slavoj Žižek, *Christian Atheism: How to Be a Real Materialist* (London, Bloomsbury, 2024), 58–62.

about Buddhism than it does about a movement typically targeting a version of world history arranged around the individual owner-subject, now seen as turning catastrophic (and soon after stabilised by the nuclear weapons regime). Žižek's model here, D.T. Suzuki, was peripheral to the Kyoto School, and is known mainly for summarising Zen for American markets. Leading Kyoto figures were actually among the most important non-European interpreters of Žižek's main model, Hegel, in whom they saw both a powerful model of dialectical thinking and a tendency to cling to the idea of the individual citizen imprinting its will on the world.[9] Kyoto writers were likely more resolutely resistant to government nudging and censorship than the average Anglosphere philosopher is today. One of the best digests of Kyoto ideas, the first of the symposia held by the journal *Chūō Kōron* right before Pearl Harbor on 26 November 1941, also doubled as a plot against the Tōjō faction.[10] This symposium is also one of the best sources of critique of a singular understanding of progress — the progress that would be held in place by the history-ending weapons then being developed and soon aimed at their recalcitrantly illiberal population.

The first *Chūō Kōron* discussion is in this sense oddly adjacent to the great critique of Enlightenment that is Theodor Adorno and Max Horkheimer's *Dialectic of Enlightenment*. Where *Dialectic of Enlightenment* points to a hidden barbarism within the singular Enlightenment's claim to have vanquished the barbaric, the nihilism behind the

---

9   David Williams argues that Kyoto's Hegel predates the 1950s French thought later seen as an origin of cultural theory: David Williams, *The Philosophy of Japanese Wartime Resistance* (Abingdon: Routledge, 2014).

10   Williams, *The Philosophy of Japanese Wartime Resistance*, xlv–xlix, liii, 57, 102.

need to cling on to a singular history, *Chūō Kōron* partici-
pants stated, led to the crisis of European authoritarianism
and the escalation of force then (though they were as yet
unaware) being readied for them in atomic form. It's not
that these writers reject modernity; rather, they stress that
in its Atlantic incarnation modernity isn't as 'modern' as
assumed. They don't deny the world based in the empiricist
self, but they think that this empiricist self is only modern
in a dialectical relation with other traditions of thought.[11]
Most urgently, the singular version of Enlightenment has
reached a nihilistic phase seen in the spread of European
fascism or, as would soon be realised, in the reliance of governments on the extinction-bound weapon.

> Capitalism, mechanized civilization, if you will, gave birth
> to imperialistic struggles such as the Great War. But it has
> also produced Europe's crisis. What perhaps, I think, should
> not have happened has happened: European civilization is
> indistinguishable from the crisis of European civilization;
> they are the same thing.[12]

If the promise of the Enlightenment had been to open
up the future, the imperial tendency to unleash Enlightenment on the world, rather than to see it as an ongoing
dialectical unfolding, meant that by the mid-twentieth
century, the open future had become fixed — thus the
alt-Hegelian call to open up Euro-American determinism.[13]

---

11   Williams, *The Philosophy of Japanese Wartime Resistance*, 120.
12   Chūō Kōron first discussion trans. David Williams, T*he
Philosophy of Japanese Wartime Resistance*, 122. Kyoto was on
the initial longlist of targets, but it was deemed not a good enough
measure of the effects of the bomb.
13   Williams, *The Philosophy of Japanese Wartime Resistance*, 128–
9. This critique could be aimed at the later Scottish Enlightenment's

Enlightenment, the *Chūō Kōron* group say (along with Adorno and Horkheimer), has been rendered unable to recognise other forms of becoming.[14] Strangely (and again despite their later caricatures), this gives them more faith in Enlightenment than Euro-Americans. They see liberalism as a powerful developmental force to be embraced, but a force that needs to dialectically open to the conditions of places that are really and substantively different: different temporalities, different *teloi*, different conceptions of the person in the social. The violence of the superweapon, they show uncannily just before the Trinity tests, marks the passage to Enlightenment as determinist: Enlightenment as a fixed authority that has to keep eviscerating its outsides. For David Williams, the subsequent cancellation of the Kyoto School by the American academy echoes this fixed *telos*, or what he calls the 'white republic', and points to an 'exhaustion of Whig history as a manifestation of liberal ethics', or a failure to maintain a moral high ground of continuous improvement and fairness through increasing measurement.[15] This is the moral collapse of a world fixed to the singular space, just as the atomic bombing of populations signals the moral collapse of the Pax Americana even as it takes on a fully world-shaping

---

tendency to fit facts onto pre-existing narratives in a 'conjectural history'. Conjectural history had been a feature of the thinking of Adam Smith scholar Dugald Stewart, whose tutees and lodgers would become some of the foremost trade and political voices behind the First Opium War, which would force the East Asian convergence with Atlantic modernity. Conjectural history's tendency to silently streamline experience for the authoritative narrative was critiqued in the *Chūō Kōron* conversation.

14   Williams, *The Philosophy of Japanese Wartime Resistance*, 126, 157.

15   Williams, *The Philosophy of Japanese Wartime Resistance*, 61.

force in 1945. The nuclear Pax Americana will try to hold off this multivocality — they will use nukes to hold it off — but for Kyoto writers like Nishida and Nishitani Keiji, the world-historical has to now be understood as a 'world of worlds', a world of self-determining places that overlap, collaborate, and develop together, but which preserve local difference against the unified space of empire.

This resistance to unified space, and the recovery of action as part of a dialectical relationship of person and environment, led Nishida to his long lingering on the term *basho*, translatable as 'place', or more widely a ground of experience and a specific structuring of space through inhabitation. In Nishida's work, physical space is not absolute and all-containing, as it had been for Newton; it is a relational field underwritten by the *basho* that localises ontology. Ultimately, a final *basho* is based in absolute nothingness/*zettai mu*, that is, standing apart from the fullness of the individual subject who had stood over the world in an attitude of evaluation. Nishida's *basho* marks an experience that is place-embedded rather than being ruled by standardised space; it derives from a mutual emptying (or kenosis) of person and place.[16] The personal depends on the historical conditions of the *basho*, which is only misguidedly understood as a vehicle for a property-structured world.[17] *Basho* pulls away from the singular abstracted development of world commercial empire, and re-opens the possibility of determination. *Basho* makes the political possible; it marks

16   John W.M. Krummel and Shigenori Nagamoto, *Place and Dialectic: Two Essays by Nishida Kitarō* (Oxford: Oxford University Press, 2012).

17   Nishida Kitarō, '*Basho*', in *Hatarakumono kara miru mono e* [*From the Working to the Watching*] (Tokyo: Iwanami, 1927 (1926)), 265–373: 266, 269; Dean Anthony Brink, *Philosophy of Science and the Kyoto School* (New York: Bloomsbury, 2021), 15.

a site of action and a site of resistance to the 'world' of Atlantic commercial empire.

Nishida's 1927 '*Basho*' essay — in fact predating Martin
Heidegger's 'Era of the World Picture' essay, which argues
for place-specificity along similar lines — is explicit in contrasting this potential of *basho* with the unified Newtonian
space that ties together all places to rob them of action.[18]
Basho resists the abstraction that places 'commercial society' and its progressive abstractions in opposition to the
embodied conflict of sword-bearers. The civilizing mission
of the space-unifying weapon then will be to denude enemies — those outside the global market — of *basho*, subjecting populations to a 'disarming', as eighteenth-century
British authorities described of Jacobites. *Basho* is a kind of
folk resistance to this totalisation. It is the obvious target
of the space-unifying weapon, in Japan as elsewhere.

This authority basis of nukes is in a way absolutely obvious: the closer you get to the local, the less support there is
for nuclear arsenals, while at higher, more abstract levels of
power, nukes are realist and normal. Shadowy peoples and
localities become repositories of access to embodied history, making them dangerous to space-unifying progress and
marking them out for extinction. The twentieth-century US
academy more or less cancelled Kyoto because they weren't
cosmopolitan enough; they weren't sufficiently obedient to
the typologies marking people out as entirely evaluable in

---

18   Kyoto School philosophers were the world's first non-German
translators of and commentators on Heidegger by decades decades,
and here Nishida precedes Heidegger's telling and comparable essay
on Newtonian space, which Kyoto thinkers would come to see as itself too bound to a fixed idea of belonging. Martin Heidegger, trans.
William Lovitt, 'The Era of The World Picture', in *The Question
Concerning Technology and Other Essays* (New York: Harper and
Row, 1977 (1938)), 115–54.

unified space — they didn't *do* race enough. If Kyoto has an ethnicity, this means an embedding in locality, and is strictly non-typological. But for the evaluative empire, anyone refusing a regime of typological value is refusing natural law and is fair game for any degree of violence (something that will be seen, on a smaller scale, in the waves of 'cancellations' that have characterised the fading days of American empire). The celebrity cancellation is banal, but behind it is the willingness to leverage indefinite violence on those who stand beyond the imperative to typologise. Or for Jean Baudrillard, 'Those who do not conceptualise difference, who do not play the game of difference, must be exterminated'.[19] The demonstration of the space-unifying weapon then becomes a template for a post-war worldwide disarming, meaning a wrenching away from *basho* as a basis of a determinable history.[20]

---

19   Williams, *The Philosophy of Japanese Wartime Resistance*, 61; Jean Baudrillard, trans. James Benedict, *The Transparency of Evil: Essays on Extreme Phenomena* (London: Verso, 2009 (1990)), 151.

20   The nihilism of race would be warned about not long after this by the most iconic theorist of decolonisation, Frantz Fanon. For Fanon's *Peau Noirs, Masques Blancs/Black Skin White Masks* (1952), racial typology, understood as a unified space of evaluation, forecloses any shared meaning and closes down any future-creating politics. Tellingly, Fanon also insists on a *physical* resistance to empire, the involvement of the body in fighting — particularly in *Les Damnés de la Terre/The Wretched of the Earth*. He does this, moreover, against an imperial power insisting on its nuclear weapons authority — Algeria's push for independence was against a France that was using the country for atomic tests at Reggane (1960–). The Algerian Sahara, like Tanizaki's shadowy interior, was non-space, and ripe for spatial disciplining. The independent Algeria emerging from this struggle would become one of the world's most important models for superpower non-alignment, as seen in the

In the US, the reception of the '45 bombings was characterised by a mixture of racialised jubilation, future shock, and trepidation at the idea of the terrible weapons ever falling into non-American hands (the impetus behind the McMahon Act of 1946). In this context, Japan was the paradigmatic model of a peripheral people who have to be returned to the one true path of modernity.[21] This would give rise to curiosities like *Our Job in Japan* (later *Design for Death* (1946/1947)), a short film by Theodor Geisel/ Dr. Seuss, liberal patriot, advocate of Japanese-American internment, and author of *The Cat in the Hat*. Lasting

---

attention paid to prime minister Ben Bella's September '62 address to the United Nations, and in the Accra assembly to follow, in which the cast for superpower non-alignment was made by Ghana's first prime minister, Kwame Nkrumah, in collaboration with Western groups including CND, at the time central to an English left protest culture. Reza Zia-Ebrahimi, 'Courting the former colony; Algeria's special position in French Third World Policy, 1963', *The Journal of North African Studies* 17–1, 2013, 23–25; Jeffrey James Byrne, *Mecca of Revolution: Algeria, Decolonization, and the Third World Order* (Oxford: Oxford University Press, 2016), 172–3, 200; Richard Taylor, *Against the Bomb: The British Peace Movement, 1958–1965 (Oxford: Clarendon, 1988*, 161–2; 8081; Stuart Hall, *NATO and the Alliances* (London: CND, 1960), 55.

21   There are various movements trying to ensure this, including the Baruch Plan (1946), which wants the US Government to effectively manage atomic technology indefinitely, and plans to more or less take over the United Nations — Paul Boyer, *By the Bomb's Early Light: American Thought and Culture at the Dawn of the Atomic Age* (New York: Pantheon, 1985), 37; Franklin, *War Stars*, 153, 164; Frederick S. Dunn, 'The Common Problem', in ed. Dunn, Bernard Brodie, Arnold Wolfers, Percy E. Corbett, and William T.R. Cox, *The Absolute Weapon: Atomic Power and World Order* (New York: Harcourt Brace, 1946), 3–17.

peace, Geisel says, is dependent on whether 'we can solve the problem of 70 million Japanese people', who 'can still make trouble, or they can make sense. We have decided to make sure they make sense'.[22] Where there have been myths 'from the ancient barbarous ages', there will now be the singular modernity made possible by the bombings. Japan itself, meanwhile, would not be seriously tempted into developing world-unifying weapons, despite a thriving nuclear energy programme. Article 9 of the Japanese Constitution stands starkly against nuclear realism (nukes as providing a seat at the top table, acting as proof of relevance, a bargaining chip, and so on). Groups centred on *hibakusha* have maintained disarmament arguments at times when they were unfashionable in Nuclear Weapons States themselves (for example, Nihon Hidankyō, eventually awarded the Nobel Peace Prize in 2024). David Cortright and Raimo Väyrynen have also suggested that the Japanese nuclear stance might show the kind of 'virtual deterrence' — there is technical ability, but assembly is complicated, and launch decisions will always be delayed beyond the panics of immediate crises.[23]

So if nukes are everywhere in the twenty-first century, it doesn't follow that every place has an equal historical stake in this form of weapon. The creation of the space-unifying weapon was founded in a specific understanding — in what we might call a Newtonian-Spenglerian expansive mission for the world. It's not that non-European powers will never have power-mad dictators (they do and they will); it's that the space-unifying weapon belongs to a specific worlding

---

22   Wr. Theodor S. Geisel and Helen Palmer, dir. Richard Fleischer, *Design for Death*, RKO, 1947.

23   David Cortright and Raimo Väyrynen, *Towards Nuclear Zero* (London: International Institute for Strategic Studies, 2010), 20, 149.

as it reaches a limit-point beyond which it can no longer adapt. It commands space as the classic imperial mission commanded space, reshaping populations' ability to think of themselves politically, even to resist the evaluative version of progress. It forces a constant adjustment to this totalisation of commercial empire, and the majority of the world's countries, including almost the whole of the southern hemisphere, don't want them.[24] Nukes then hang around as the attritional form of an older claim to a singular development, with the Japanese bombing as the paradigmatic example of this. The nukes see off any threats of *basho* or embodied action, seeping into the population's everyday expectations and prising individuals out of their locales.

---

24   The 2017 Treaty on the Prohibition of Nuclear Weapons (TPNW) was signed by almost the entirety of the Global South, and disregarded by Nuclear Weapons States and NATO – ICAN. Text of the Treaty on the Prohibition on Nuclear Weapons, 2017: https://www.icanw.org/tpnw_full_text

FOLK *BASHO* AND
PRE-NUCLEAR GHOSTS

Basho is a helpful way of describing what nuclear empire wants to destroy. *Basho*, the plane of experience connected to real, mutable bodies in historically determined places, might be understood as the interruption of abstracted violence. *Basho* resists the transcendental violence concretised in the 'worldly' weapon. As Orwell intuited, atomic weapons enact a shift of authority upwards to rise above the resistance of highly surveilled populations with no access to the means of conflict. Or, as Raymond Williams put it, populations governed by nuclear arsenals 'become objects in an ideology of deterrence determined by interests wholly beyond us as nations or as peoples'.[1] *Basho* is a grounding for social stakes underneath this nuclear tendency to, as Scarry puts it, 'delete the population'.[2] The liberalism backed by the superweapon formally liberates populations — they come to be made up of self-actualising individuals free from barbaric violence — but also has them internalise a position of defencelessness and isolation *contra* liberalism's promises. For E.P. Thompson, a New Left fellow-traveler of Williams and perhaps the best-known anti-nuclear campaigner of the Cold War era, the amassing of nuclear arsenals marks a stage at which capitalist development slips the anchor of

---

1   Williams, 'The Politics of Nuclear Disarmament', 33.
2   Scarry, *Thermonuclear Monarchy*, 35.

any utility and begins to act autonomously, a stage at which impulses towards democratic solidarity come to 'appear as hideous threats to established power'.[3] For Michael Foot — speaking at the 1960 Aldermaston March and echoing C. Wright Mills's recent description of nuclear technocracies as 'military dictatorships' — the abstracted authority of nuclear arsenals is 'in permanent session, beyond the reach of elections, votes, and governments'.[4] The deterrent is always busy progressively removing political determinability. Running in the other direction is a tradition of folk politics that passes through Foot to millennial hauntological writing's focus on the agency of the specific place. Scepticism towards nuclear weapons authority is a defining feature of this thread of folk or *basho* politics, though this tradition has rarely been acknowledged as having a nuclear element.

If the concept of *basho* started its life in an environment where some everyday animism or entanglement with place could be assumed — Japan — it also fits onto a hinterland of English ecology, onto a tradition of place-embedded lived-experience. English anti-nuclear action itself has always been strongly bound up with localism: for the official nuclear historian Beatrice Heuser, the early Campaign for Nuclear Disarmament (CND) was a 'classical folk or grassroots movement', and in its early years from the late '50s, it may have been *the* primary source of English folk resistance.[5] Actions surrounding CND pushed it away from parliamentary and similar allegiances — it stood apart from the post-war technocracy approved by the Labour Party —

3   Thompson, 'Notes on Exterminism, the Last Stage of Civilization', Thompson, *Exterminism and Cold War*, 1–33: 25

4   Richard Taylor, *Against the Bomb: The British Peace Movement, 1958–1965* (Oxford: Clarendon, 1988), 8.

5   Beatrice Heuser, *Nuclear Mentalities: Strategies and Beliefs in Britain, France, and the FRG* (Basingstoke: Palgrave, 1998), 14.

and it often overlapped with various threads of a New Left galvanised by the Soviet Union's moral catastrophes and which advocated non-alignment with both superpowers (at times being described as 'CND's thinktank'). Non-alignment movements drew on English folk resources and mobilised what Richard Taylor calls a 'moral nationalism... the rights of free individuals and free nations to determine their futures'.[6] If this kind of national non-alignment was largely buried by the American universalism of the millennial culture wars, it's worth remembering how central it once was to an anti-imperial English left. Between 1958 and 1961, the Aldermaston Marches were genuine mass movements and involved countless spin-off union and university events. In 1960, CND were able to press the Labour Party at their Scarborough conference into a unilateralist pledge, even if it only lasted a year.[7]

Something similar was true of the Scottish 'localism' that would feed into independence movements originating largely as resistance to nuclear authority. In 1961, the housing of American nukes at Holy Loch galvanised a rising national consciousness and constitutional scepticism.[8] Pan-British localism was crucial even to making the nuclear threat thinkable, to stopping it completely taking its place as an insivible realism. During the 'New Cold War' (the revival of nuclear danger in 1979–86), and against the background of Margaret Thatcher's suppression of local government, numerous local authorities declared themselves nuclear-free zones in areas including Glasgow, Leeds,

---

6   Taylor, *Against the Bomb*, 305, 331–3.

7   Taylor, *Against the Bomb*, 43, 58, 78–79.

8   A rising philosophical counter-dualism was also important to this; throughout the 1950s, Scottish academic philosophers had been struggling to overcome analytic philosophy, and approached Heidegger long after Kyoto, but long before the rest of the UK.

Manchester and Sheffield (providing one reason for the decision to locate the Cold War's best-known drama of nuclear war, *Threads*, in that city). The nuclear-free local authority was easy enough to laugh at, and was often caricatured as demanding that Soviet missiles observe current British administrative boundaries. But more than this, local nuclear-free status was a reminder of how the threat effectively managed populations, and at times helped keep alive the impetus to model real nuclear emergencies whose details might otherwise have been fudged by official messaging (as happened in Sheffield itself).[9] Local-authority discontent also had had real consequences, including the cancellation of the 1982 NATO exercise 'Hard Rock'. Anglo-localism was crucial to keeping nuclear violence thinkable, and is still a key to denaturalising nukes.

One obvious difference between Scottish localism and English localism is that English localism tends to have no real ambitions to a national platform, where Scottish pan-localism has a political national presence acting as a real irritant to British deterrent authority. Some (like me) have pressed 'English nation versus British state' arguments, originally for Tom Nairn–type reasons about adapting Scottish ideas of self-determination to the local centre of British ideology, and the twenty-first century English inheritors of the non-alignment tradition of Stuart Hall or Raymond Williams have had some sympathy with this. Easy to brush off in the 2010s as an identity question — as a question that can itself be reduced to the criterion of measurement — English independence still has a real political import, and still needs to face down accusations of eternal Toryhood (the psephological assumption that an English polity would always point Conservative). In any

---

9   Julie McDowall, *Attack Warning Red!: How Britain Prepared for Nuclear War* (London: Vintage, 2024), 96.

case, the question of an English 'cohesive national identity' has often puzzled those Scots who tend to see questions of independence as part of the normal process for overhauling an entropic constitution, one whose continuity predisposes it to the permanent presence of extinction-level weapons.

It's true that Anglo-indy remains a thought experiment to some extent, but it might also be understood as a set of transitional demands — demands that fit the official stances of progressive British institutions, but the impossibility of fulfilling which reveals certain contradictions, not least the promise to deliver security through indefinite nuclear standoff. English *basho* can be simultaneously national and a staging-post in driving sovereignty downwards. Anglo-localism entails a movement away from the abstraction of natural/nuclear law, and towards ecological entanglements with places with living memories. This is one reason early CND and the Hall-Williams sections of the New Left echo in hauntology, with its concern with the kinds of memory and agency specific to places (rather than those absorbed by the Newtonian individualism of absolute space). Fisher's description of how places become 'stained' with memory closely parallels a kind of English *basho*. The appeal of the folk horror or folk revival recovered by hauntology is in its commitment to 'placedness' amid the space totalised by the reach of nukes over all life, and insisting on rational property-owning individuals standing apart from landscape.[10]

---

10   Mark Fisher, 'The Slow Cancellation of the Past', *Ghosts of My Life: Writings on depression, hauntology and lost futures* (Winchester: Zer0, 2014), 26–28. Conversely, Tanizaki Jun'ichirō's house interior, somewhat animist like the environments of classic English folk horror, is 'stained' in much the way Fisher describes — it contains the opaque ghosts of ancestors accepted as real presences. This account of housebuilding to escape Tokyo consumerism is a digest of light-interrupting technologies, dark foods, haptic media,

If the stuff of folk horror looks spooky or animistic, it's because it hasn't yet been prised out of its environment by the empire of light. Its weird agency is in its concealment from the perfect abstraction of the nuclear regime.

Thus classic folk horror's struggle with automation, or the singular line of progress that rejects all human interference and which often, like *Chūō Kōron*, indicates an extinction unconscious, or a deep acceptance of the progressive eclipse of biological life. In the 1975 TV adaptation of John Christopher's *Weathermonger* children's fiction trilogy, retitled *The Changes*, the population is seized by a fear of machines, and flee their homes in nomadic tribes, leaving a trail of broken kettles and toasters behind them. Their instinct is right, of course, and should be remembered for the labour-cutting nihilism of the self-service checkout. At the *Weathermonger* point in the career of folk horror, the dawn of neoliberal automation is bringing into focus fears of human eclipse, but behind this are the extinction systems that apparently unavoidably 'delete the population'. The folk horror of this period is also full of stories of people negotiating civilisational collapse and having to reset time — displaced apocalypses — and asking how to negotiate newly primitive conditions. In Terry Nation's *Survivors* (1975), a pandemic introduces instant depopulation and a long meditation on how anything might be made by hand — bread from wheat, wheat from ploughing, ploughs from forging, forging from smelting; behind this lies the boom in self-sufficiency and the sense that only local knowledge can answer an apocalypse imposed on a global level. Folk horror's gnarly issues of self-sufficiency echo on in the nuclear war dramas of the next decade, as in the opening sequence of *Threads*, which sees a spider weave a web against

---

and *shoji*/screen doors that produce translucence and interrupt fields of vision and ownership.

a Sheffield backdrop while a voiceover reminds us that 'in an urban society, everything connects. Each person's needs are met by the skills of many others. Our lives are woven together in a fabric. But the connections that make society strong also make it vulnerable'.[11] In the great drama of *basho* versus nukes *Edge of Darkness* (1985), a detective is led by the spectral presence of his dead daughter from a West Yorkshire farmhouse through the anonymous spaces of the London establishment, ending in his *becoming ecological* by dissolving into a Scottish mountainside. Finally the division of self and environment is overcome, the anthropocentric assumption becomes redundant and the nuclear empire defending the property-owning self collapses.[12]

Nuclear threat, then, is perhaps the missing element of English folk politics — something that might have been less surprising to the earnest kitchen-sinkery of CND in 1959. In other words, the period when nuclear weapons realism was recognised as a site of political contest was also the period of the autonomy of *basho* before the great neoliberal flattening, and the classic era of popular folk horror. The nuclear issue has almost never come up in hauntological writing, although

---

11   Wr. Barry Hines, dir. Mick Jackson, *Threads* (BBC/Nine, 1984).

12   A lot of hauntological writing on folk horror hints at stones' comprising a disorientingly long sweep, one beyond human comprehension; the familiarly cult children's TV series *Children of the Stones*, describing the occult time-warping power of a stone circle, gave its name to the geeky salutation of folk horror enthusiasts, 'Happy Day'. Similar for the 1979 version of the BBC series *Quatermass*. In Scotland, where *Edge of Darkness*'s Craven ends up, and where Kennedy Martin is from, there is an even stronger association of animistic stones as markers of time travel; Stonehenge equivalents in places like Callanish or Grampian pepper twentieth-century Scottish writing and helped define independence.

the possibility of meaningful place connects them. As it happens, folk horror does find a home in at least one classic nuclear fiction — Russell Hoban's *Riddley Walker*, published in 1980, written in the late '70s. In Hoban's post-apocalyptic psychogeography of Kent, a group of boys work their way across localities whose substrates contain ancient memories of defence technology and clues as to the history that progressed from explosives to thermonuclear weapons, and might do so again. The names of these localities appear as comic corruptions, showing the failure of the ideal representation the space-unifying weapon is supposed to protect (Dover is 'Do It Over'; Wittersham is 'Widders Dump'). Here, nuclear weapons are both the destination of technological advance and a talismanic folk horror — the 'Eusa story' that brings the great light, the 'shyning' that leaves the boys wondering about the inevitability of the return to nuclear standoff and questioning how hardwired their 'extinction destiny' really is.[13]

How inevitable really, Hoban's adolescent walkers ask, is the perpetual rise to apocalypse? Are there versions of history buried in these Kentish places? As it happens, children had been asking this in nuclear apocalypse for a while. John Wyndham's *The Chrysalids* (1955), for example, one of the ur-texts of folk horror, and a novel in which struggling Labradorians (acting extremely English), ruled by a new puritan fear regarding genetic mutation exercise constant vigilance for the unnatural — a kind of witch-hunting. Wyndham's children discover telepathic abilities triggered by radiation-driven mutations and have to try to hide their world-reshaping abilities from puritanical adults — though we suspect their abilities will break the historiographical order and create a more empathetic world. The distant

---

13   Russell Hoban, *Riddley Walker* (London: Penguin, 2021 (1980)).

telepaths, it turns out, are in what was once New Zealand — a longstanding trope in nuclear fiction that places the antipodes beyond a nuclearised north which has burned out its own moral mission and been dumped back into premodern superstition. The 'nuclear mutant telepath' itself would remain a fairly common trope in the '60s and '70s as the inevitability of extinction was interrogated. 'Future-creating telepathic kids' would even become a staple of the kind of kids' TV that extensively intersects with Fisher-type folk horror: *Chocky*, *Children of the Stones*, *The Tomorrow People*. ('Let the children lose it/Let the children use it/Let the children boogie', as Bowie did *not* paraphrase *The Tomorrow People* — Bowie was a year earlier). These are archaeologies of knowledge looking for a kind of 'time travel' to undo the inexorable trudge towards nuclear rule; and they all rely on a relationship to English place outstripping the imperative to evaluate and own.

English place, then, should be understood as a central part of the nuclear imagination. It has a role in making the stakes of nuclear threat thinkable within the British authority that naturalised it. Emplaced versions of Englishness cut open the imperatives of nuclear security; hauntology spots this, as does a twenty-first century tradition of art describing how radiation has entered the landscape, as in the *Cumbrian Alchemy* project (2012–14), layering stone, industry, and long-half-life radionuclides. Numerous millennial versions of a new Englishness, in visions as far apart as the progressive northern federalism of Alex Niven and the eco-folkishness of Paul Kingsnorth, are basically post-nuke, either with no time for deterrence or positively rejecting it. (Apparently 'divisive' for some, Kingsnorth was also an editor of the magazine at the heart of the '70s self-sufficiency movement, the *Ecologist*). Why, it could be objected, would nukes ever be paraded as part of an inspiring vision? But their absence itself suggests how more *basho*-oriented accounts tend to bracket some of the most cherished tenets of British inertia, pulling sovereignty away from abstraction, pulling the country away from extinction realism. This kind of account of English place is solidly post-British — whether or not it's said so explicitly — and it triggers a deep nuclear weapons scepticism. Nukes are deeply intertwined with British authority; without one, the other falls away. On a UK level, nukes are almost too obvious to think; on a local or even an English level, nukes almost never come up. The eternal British state needs history-arresting weapons; folk politics sees this arrest of history as a kind of repeating disaster. Or in language more palatable to the Labour thinktanks who entertained Anglo-indy briefly in the 2010s, the nuclear imagination is an imagination of constitutional reform, and vice-versa. Fill in the empty abstraction that is 'the British nation', and naturalised nukes are in trouble. The problem is that post-war technocracy made this abstraction so fundamental that it was often gratefully embraced as fundamental to a socialist vision of wellbeing, or as a patriotic element of the welfare state, financially rational and utterly secure — nukes as cheap extinction.

CHEAP EXTINCTION

In Britain at least, the moment when the nuclear regime really finally eclipsed any citizen interference in the shaping and protection of society can be dated pretty specifically at the height of the post-war consensus. The government was already heavily committed to deterrence when hydrogen bombs took over the deterrence landscape in the mid-1950s — the US's Ivy Mike test in November 1952; the Soviet RDS37 test in November 1955; the UK's Grapple X test in November 1957. The push for superweapons was already decades long. Building on intense research into nuclear fission, concrete research into viable atomic weapons had begun across UK universities at the start of the '40s. Particularly after the 1940 Frisch-Peierls memorandum, an already extensive and prestigious aerospace industry took on atomic technology as part of its missions to restore pride, and after an initial shock, nuclear motifs suffused official post-war cultures, seen for example in the 1951 Festival of Britain at the South Bank. Smaller provincial festivals for those who couldn't make it to London often featured exhibits on preparation for nuclear war.[1] It had been

1   David Edgerton, *England and the Aeroplane : Militarism, Modernity, and Machines* (London: Penguin, 2013), 28, 66; Samuel J. M. M. Alberti et al, *Cold War Scotland* (Edinburgh: NMSE, 2024), 27; Lawrence Freedman, *Britain and Nuclear Weapons* (London: Macmillan, 1980), 3; McDowall, *Attack Warning Red!*, 144.

British research, via the co-ordinating MAUD Committee, that had convinced the Americans about the need for the atomic weapon, with the result that exceptionalist Britain was relegated to being an American client state.[2] The boffin state promised an atomic energy revolution, but, as Wells might have described, this energy revolution was itself predicated on nuclear weapons manufacturing. One open secret about the rebuilding of the post-war UK is that power stations including Windscale, Chapelcross, and Calder Hall — opened in 1956 with the iconic image of a new Queen standing before an electricity meter supposedly counting kilowatt-hours (in fact unconnected) — were primarily there to produce weapons-grade plutonium.[3] The imagery of post-war belonging is suffused with this kind of top-down nuclear triumphalism.

In the US, meanwhile, the '45 bombings had been key to the affirmation of the progressive Atlantic mission. For the *Nation*, the bombing of populations 'moves humanity forward several centuries'; for the *New York Times* it was 'but a sample' of more to come.[4] But if Americans imagined strategic atomic strikes to extend their geopolitical influence, the British took all-out deterrence more literally. For one thing, Western Europe was a likely atomic front line. But the ideal of absolute defence also had roots deep in British mythology. Its authority supposedly given by nature and empirically demonstrable, as in in the tradition of Newton and Locke, Britain was presented as always raising law over naked power (feeding into the ideal of 'NATO neutrality').

---

2   Rodric Braithwaite, *Armageddon and Paranoia: The Nuclear Confrontation* (London: Profile, 2017), 52.

3   The queen, dignitaries, and boffins look gravely at the moving metre, though its readout is obviously unrealistic: youtube.com/watch?v=ey9envpF_TE

4   Boyer, *By the Bomb's Early Light*, 134, 13, 19, 129.

Pure defensiveness had been a principle of cohesion during the Blitz, a morale-boosting affirmation of moral rightness, and formed the backdrop against which the MAUD Committee met.[5] At the end of British empire, defence had become part of a psychology of resilience and patriotic rebuilding. Even during the original 'austerity' made virtuous by Labour's 1947 budget, the Clement Attlee government committed to spending as much as it could on the nuclear arsenal without *overtly* seeming to re-enter a war condition.[6] Even though he understood that the UK was in the atomic firing line, this architect of the welfare state reasoned that 'the answer to an atomic bomb on London is an atomic bomb on another great city'.[7] Nukes were bound up with collective effort, absolute defence, homeliness, sociality.

Perpetual nuclear threat, then, has always been strangely comforting in the UK. It has also always been taken as a kind of democratisation, turning the whole population into combatants. Nukes were the home front of a terminal war, and a crux of what would come to be called inclusion. They involved an ever greater percentage of the population, raising the likely civilian proportion of total estimated deaths above 95%, capping a climb in this proportion since the late

---

5 England had also been the first country to be hit by ballistic missiles, in the form of V2 rockets: Matthew Jones, *The Official History of the UK Strategic Nuclear Deterrent, Volume I: From the V-Bomber Era to the Arrival of Polaris* (Abingdon: Routledge, 2017), 5.

6 Andrew Pierre, *Nuclear Politics: The British experience with an independent strategic force, 1939–1970* (London: Oxford University Press, 1972), 86.

7 Len Scott and Stephen Twigge, *Britain, the United States and the Command of Western Nuclear Forces* (Abingdon: Routledge, 2000).

nineteenth century. Nukes didn't mark a disappearance of physical war — physical war would definitely still be with us — but they did suggest a greater abstraction of war's ultimate threat to the population. Welfare technocracy democratically turned populations into deterrence stakeholders, but at the same time it reserved decisions on apocalyptic force to tiny secret committees (Attlee's GEN 75, initially). The absorption of desires for inclusion collapsed the question of mass extinction into a logic of competitiveness filtered through supposedly neutral electoral machinery. In this democratisation, democracy is terminally degraded, since it's impossible for enough information to circulate about the conditions of nuclear war decision-making or preparation. Nukes, as numerous commentators have described, ultimately make democracy impossible, or mark its disappearance.

But through the lens of British consensus, nuclear violence — fully abstracted violence — was fair, it was gentle and modern, it was a form of security given to the people as reward for the war effort, and as much a pillar of the welfare state as the NHS or Social Security.[8] If the welfare state makes people healthier and more secure, it also makes them more valuable as nuclear targets.[9] On a British level, the terminology of welfare security and nuclear security have always been entwined. In 2024, Keir Starmer was still promising that under an incoming Labour government, the Trident nuclear weapons system would be protected by a 'triple lock' — a term previously used with regard to state pensions.[10] Despite the immediate post-election

---

8   James, *The Official History of the UK Strategic Nuclear Deterrent, Volume I*, 2; Heuser, *Nuclear Mentalities*, 20.

9   McDowall, *Attack Warning Red!*, 56.

10   Nick Ritchie, 'Keir Starmer's Trident triple lock', *The Conversation*, 6 June 2024: theconversation.com/keir-starmers-tri-

warnings of the terrible financial decisions to be made by Starmer's government to combat a £22bn 'black hole' in the accounts, not only was the £200bn-lifespan Trident system so exempt that it was barely mentioned, nuclear weapons expansion would even become a kind of balm for the economy, promising growth and revived public services. Nuclear securitisation could be slotted into the a naturalistic language of rights that put it before any political opinion: for Margaret Gowing, nuclear deterrence was 'fundamental and almost instinctive'; for Nick Ritchie, it was unimpeachable due to its 'underpinning Britain's core self-identity as a major "pivotal" power'.[11] When, in the '50s, the H-bomb promised to truly 'delete the population', multiplying yields by a factor of around 100, it merely affirmed existing democratic assumptions and found its place in the homely realism of the post-war consensus, attracting little parliamentary debate. The terrible violence of H-bomb allowed spending cuts for shelters and fighting; its status as the unstrategisable allowed a public image of gentleness to persist; it promised geopolitical prestige, at least if the 'independent' deterrent was taken at face value; and it was instrumental to a post-war technocratic restructuring and the backbone of the post-war consensus.

By the end of the 1950s, cheap extinction had become the only story acceptable across British parliament, leaving scepticism to the tweedier margins. The key architects of the welfare state remained solidly behind it, with the

---

dent-triple-lock-how-britains-obsession-with-nuclear-weapons-has-become-part-of-election-campaigns-231834.

11   Margaret Gowing, *Independence and Deterrence: Britain and Atomic Energy, 1945–1952, Volume 1* (London: Macmillan, 1974), 184; Nick Ritchie, *Trident and British Identity: Letting Go of Nuclear Weapons* (Bradford: University of Bradford, 2008), 12.

leadership of the 1950s–60s Labour Party dedicating much energy to fighting off disarming tendencies within the rank and file.[12] By the end of the '50s, Nye Bevan was moving strongly against unilateralists, in part because of realist worries about losing global prestige, in part for the more banal reason that he needed union support to become foreign secretary (cheap apocalypse often defaulting to the needs of individual senior politicians like this).[13] In the quietly top-heavy system anchored by GEN 75 and its successors, the ability to deliver savings with which to shore up future spending promises created a bureaucratic momentum that pushed sceptical voices beyond the parliamentary pale. Thus, the role of the New Left would be defined in part by their commitment to non-alignment, independence from American and Soviet nuclear empires, and an understanding of nuclear threat as being wagered not between rival peoples but by a particular state form over the population. Stuart Hall, later known as a pioneer of Cultural Studies and left scepticism, described a non-aligned independence of mind in this way in 1960:

Britain, DISENCUMBERED OF BOTH BOMB AND ALLIANCE, would then be free to act as a rallying point outside both nuclear alliances — the Warsaw Pact and NATO: a focus for all those other nations, within and without both nuclear alliances, which could be persuaded by the weight of international opinion, to join an offensive for disengagement and disarmament. The postures of

---

12   John Baylis and Kristan Stoddart, *The British Nuclear Experience: The Roles of Beliefs, Culture and Identity* (Oxford: Oxford University Press, 2015), 16–41; Jacques E.C. Hymans, *The Psychology of Nuclear Proliferation: Identity, Emotions and Foreign Policy* (Cambridge: Cambridge University Press, 2006).

13   Taylor, *Against the Bomb*, 19, 278.

the Cold War can only be broken up by a country moving horizontally across a landscape frozen vertically into two camps.[14]

Familiarly, ideas of non-alignment would be killed off by superpowers, in a dynamic worth remembering in the 'third nuclear era'. As Hall was writing, the US government was engaging in the greatest nuclear arming in history, largely justified by the mythology of the 'missile gap', the assumption that the Soviet Union had pulled ahead in nuclear firepower. Heavily lobbied by aerospace companies like Boeing and Lockheed, politicians made pitches to Congress for as much nuclear funding as possible, rather than what they thought was needed — meaning that the massive overkill normalised in the US's great era of prosperity had more to do with the 'art of the deal' than with population requirements. President Eisenhower's epochal January '61 speech on the 'military-industrial complex', echoing C. Wright Mills's *The Causes of World War Three* (1958), drew praise from Hall and others in the New Left, despite coming from a Republican president.[15] The Democrat John F. Kennedy had used the missile gap myth to promise security during his 1960 presidential campaign (coming to a head two years later in the Cuban Missile Crisis); from January 1961, Kennedy's defence secretary, Robert McNamara, massively overbid for nukes and further angled the targeting of warheads towards civilian populations — setting up a condition in which the world could be held to ransom by the economic imperatives of a booming American empire. By the mid-1960s, an extraordinary 20000 Mt of warheads had been built up in the US, largely through corporate cap-

---

14   Hall, *NATO and the Alliances*, 5.
15   C. Wright Mills, *The Causes of World War Three* (New York: Simon and Schuster, 1958).

ture, and largely targeted at civilian populations. As Benoît Pelopidas asks, if the Atlantic 1960s has been culturally associated with liberation, should it instead be associated with the kind of No-Future condition we now know from the inception of '70s neoliberalism? In other words, 'did a similar attempt at closing the future happen with nuclear weapons a decade earlier?'[16]

Despite signalling about an independent British deterrent — Bevan's famous insistence that the British bomb had 'to have a bloody union jack on it' — this massive American arsenal was one factor in making the UK a helpless recipient of American soft power. Thus the extraordinary and exhausting spread, over this long period from the 1950s to the 2020s, of American values to its transatlantic satellite: American network TV; English kids singing American rock about American places; moral panics over American celebrities; obsession over American elections; moral lessons imported from the world's most expensive universities; and eventually, the flooding of the English political space by American cultural wars, with young Europeans drafted into a kind of pan-Atlantic national service. The UK of the thermonuclear Pax Americana might come to be seen as the East Germany of the American empire, except that the control gets even stronger after the Cold War. We might describe the demand that English youth keep emotionally investing in American dramas of public virtue as 'A Clockwork Orange in reverse' — the mirror image of the Soviet infiltration imagined by Anthony Burgess's 1962 novel, sinking into

---

16   Quoted in Benoît Pelopidas, 'The Birth of Nuclear Eternity', in eds. Sandra Kemp and Jenny Andersson, *Futures* (Oxford: Oxford University Press, 2021), 484–500', 484.

the wider culture and kids' speech — 'most of the roots are Slav. Propaganda. Subliminal penetration'.[17]

Nevertheless, the early thermonuclear era helped usher in a patriotic welfarism in Britain, held in place by a technocratic consensus always gradually jettisoning its population. If the government had realised as early as 1949 that a comprehensive shelter programme was prohibitively expensive, the development of H-bombs absolutely affirmed this shift in defence.[18] A breakwater came with the epochal Strath Report of 1955, describing the impact of a modest ten Soviet bombs and describing, in level-headed civil service language, how meaningful protection was economically impossible and the population would effectively be held up for sacrifice. A number of local councils had recently begun to refuse the performance of shelter building, which they recognised as pointless. Matthew Grant describes the situation of Coventry City Council, where

> on 5 April [1954] the Labour controlled local authority passed a resolution declaring that 'in view of the recent reports in regard to the explosion of the hydrogen bomb and its devastating effects', it would inform the Home Secretary that 'it is a waste of public time and money to carry on with the Civil Defence Committee: therefore, it is the Council's intention to take steps to terminate its existence'.[19]

---

17   Anthony Burgess, *A Clockwork Orange* (London: Penguin, 2000 (1962)), 86.

18   Matthew Grant, 'Home Defence and the Sandys White Paper, 1957', *Journal of Strategic Studies* 31–6, 2008: core.ac.uk/download/pdf/16387567.pdf

19   Matthew Grant, *After the Bomb: Civil Defence and Nuclear War in Britain, 1945–68* (Basingstoke: Palgrave, 2010), 78.

The new reality is confirmed by the Defence White Paper of 1957, which described how 'it must be frankly admitted that there is at present no means of providing adequate protection for the people of this country against the consequences of an attack with nuclear weapons'.[20] Policy would now shrink to warning plus counter-strike, the aim being 'no longer to defend the population against aerial attack but to defend the deterrent and provide sufficient warning to enable HMG to launch a retaliatory nuclear strike'.[21] As Hall put it, there had been an admission that 'Britain was not equipped to fight any other but a nuclear war', but also that the nuclear war was an ongoing psychological war fought for public perception — 'The nuclear deterrent is no longer essentially a matter of military strategy, but much more a question of vague but dangerous psychological reassurances'.[22]

In this situation, a previous official duty to protect the population had to be squared with an increasingly overt and virtuous defencelessness — one that valued cost-cutting on shelters and soldiers' labour, and so could be seen as patriotic. For Attlee, trying to defend the population would itself undermine deterrence: it 'would cause the population

20   Ministry of Defence, *Defence: Outline of Future Policy* (London: MoD, 1957), 2.

21   Richard Moore, *Nuclear Illusion, Nuclear Reality: Britain, the United States and Nuclear Weapons, 1958–64* (Basingstoke: Palgrave, 2010), 27, 77, 240, 250; Scott and Twigge, *Planning Armageddon*, 92, 288; A.J.R. Groom, *British Thinking About Nuclear Weapons* (London: F. Pinter, 1974), 201; Jones, *The Official History of the UK Strategic Nuclear Deterrent, Volume I*, 46, 102, 122.

22   Stuart Hall, *NATO and the Alliances*, 3.

to rest easy... and actually invite the destruction offensive preparations were hoping to avoid'.[23] As Grant says,

> [Attlee] feared that the public might clamour for preparations the government could not afford. Attlee himself delivered a telling statement, that... it was... essential to avoid a situation in which the Government would be driven to devote resources to civil defence on a scale which would cripple the national economy.[24]

Shelter, then, is paradoxically dangerous: it under-mines the security of Mutually Assured Destruction, which needs the constant barter of a prone population, while our 'national' wellbeing depends on not thinking too overtly about shelter reality. The nuclear imagination, then, has to imagine not a population sheltered, but one prevented from making the question of shelters too ob-vious. Grant describes 'a continual fear throughout the atomic age that public clamour might force a government into adopting a ruinously expensive civil defence policy, and this fear greatly influenced the government's attitude to civil defence publicity'.[25] The nuclear battle, then, was less a physical battle than a cultural one, a battle over the thinkability of the authority of nuclear weapons; and civil defence policy was in the tricky position of having to pres-ent a patrician outlook while avoiding too much inquiry into the real effectiveness of shelters. Spending on civil defence would have to become highly visible and improve morale even as it became obviously pointless — a façade that would lead on to a now-familiar cultural condition of cognitive dissonance.

---

23   Grant, *After the Bomb*, 42.
24   Grant, *After the Bomb*, 32.
25   Grant, *After the Bomb*, 32.

A performative civil defence, often seemingly stuck in Blitz mode, would turn into a strangely comforting camp, an atavistic sign of hopeless patriotism, a *Carry On Extinction*. In official civil defence messaging, round-hatted volunteers pointed firehoses at megaton blasts, stretching out a cohesive ideology of British security and providing a kind of disjunctive morale boosting, against which activists' work to raise awareness of the population's being primed for barter in nuclear standoff would become an important element of a growing counterculture.[26] In 1963, a government bunker near Reading was entered by Spies for Peace, an activist group adjacent to CND's civil disobedience Committee of 100. The Committee of 100 included Stuart Hall and Bertrand Russell; Spies for Peace likely included Michael Randle (co-organiser of the pan-African anti-nuclear conference that followed Algerian independence), the anarchist philosopher April Carter, and Russell's mentor on nuclear weapons issues, Ralph Schoeman — with sympathisers including the great narrator of British slow collapse, Doris Lessing, E.P. Thompson, and the pop philosopher John Berger, known for his TV introduction of Walter Benjamin's ideas on art and mass production, *Ways of Seeing*. In the Reading bunker, Spies for Peace found documents, plans, maps and personnel lists, copied for the pamphlet *Danger! Official Secret: RSG-6*, which was distributed at the Aldermaston rally.[27] This pamphlet showed that official plans clearly prioritised military government over populations and vested power in a 'group of people who have accepted thermonuclear war as a probability, and are consciously and actively planning for it'. It described

---

26 Grant, *After the Bomb*, 8–9.
27 Spies for Peace, *Danger! Official Secret: RSG6*, 1963, reproduced at: files.libcom.org/files/DANGER_OFFICIAL_SECRET_RSG-6.pdf

the locations of ten existing Regional Seats of Government (RSGs) — Catterick, York, Nottingham, Cambridge, Reading, Edinburgh, Dartmouth, Brecon, Kidderminster, Preston, Dover, Armagh — and opened its description of the Reading facility with a passage that could have come from a folk-horror-era *Play for Today*:

> The entrance to RSG-6 is a few yards across the road from the Red House pub, at the east end of Warren Row. It is surrounded and masked by thick woods and low hills. All that can be seen from the road is a padlocked wooden gate and a gatekeeper's hut. There is no name outside, and no indication that it is a Government establishment. It has been crudely but effectively disguised...

In an emergency, people were 'told to get in 14 days' supply of food and water (where from?), and to stay under cover for seven days (then what?)'. Large, heavily populated areas like London were called 'Z-zones' and abandoned. Although this information had to be kept from the domestic population at all costs, it was common knowledge to an international nuclear class managing their unproductive classes through nuclear threat: 'You can be sure the Russian Government knows all about it. You can be sure the American Government knows all about it. The British people are *meant to know nothing at all*'. The British constitution here collapses, folk horror-style, into a kind of feudal barbarism ruled by post-nuclear chieftains — like Councillor Sutton in *Threads*, hastily drafted in to the Sheffield bunker where he will be immured at his post — joined by an arcane collection of British establishment figures:

> Virtually every important Government department except the Church of England is represented and has been given its staff and offices. There are rooms for the Army, Navy,

Air Force, Police, Fire Brigade and Civil Defence. Each of these is centralised under a Supremo, who has already been named in each case. There are offices for the Treasury (including the Big Five), the Central Office of Information, the GPO, the BBC (but not ITV!), the Board of Trade, and the Ministries of Health, Food, Supply, Transport and Power. Other departments will undoubtedly be important after the Bomb drops, and which also have offices in RSG-6, are the Ministry of Labour, the National Assistance Board, and the WVS.

The functions of the various government departments are enlightening. The COI will be responsible for censorship, as well as for public announcements (to whom?). The Ministry of Labour will be responsible for conscription of special workers, as well as for labour relations (between whom?). The Ministry of Housing will deal with the disposal of the dead as well as the homeless. There are offices too for departments without analogous peacetime functions. Thus the Scientific Unit will deal with bomb data and radiation risks, and HMSO will print and publish proclamations against rioting.[28]

The late 1950s to early '60s saw this great turn inwards to the comfort of the earth, away from the outward push of evolution, understood as a limit point for the species. For Paul Virilio's *Bunker Archaeology* (1958) the bunker is a crypt where the doomed wait for resurrection.[29] The bunker points towards mere survival, 'life without liveliness' (Peter Sloterdijk), an end of meaning. Even when protected from thermonuclear evisceration, the person falls away from the world, losing any stake in the social, as Scarry

---

28   Spies for Peace, *Danger! Official Secret*.
29   Paul Virilio, *Bunker Archaeology* (New York: Princeton University Press, 1994 (1958)).

would describe. In Daniel Galouye's *Dark Universe* (1961), a blind people burrowing underground learn to navigate by sound and smell, and develop a strange mythology of light as redemption.[30] With the Partial Test Ban Treaty in 1963 driving testing itself underground, populations were left burrowing towards comfort within a planet doomed to entropic destruction.[31] The condition of constant performative pseudo-war backing Atlantic prosperity now gave rise to stories of shelter-as-ideology, as in Philip K. Dick's 1964 novel *The Penultimate Truth*, in which humanity, forced underground, is allowed to believe in a real war while a surface elite use nuclear threat to exploit the labour of the subterranean population.[32] Adam Piette describes how Project Sunshine — a large-scale investigation into the effects of nuclear war — focused attention on an underground eternity, and sees this in Samuel Beckett's 1964 'All Strange Away', a short text in which an incarcerated protagonist is subjected to a 'hot glare'.[33] This 'hot glare' might in turn remind us of the shopping arcades of Tanizaki's *In Praise of Shadows*, from which the dweller in the shadowy house looks for shelter; and it will

---

30   Daniel F. Galouye, *Dark Universe* (London: Gollancz, 2000 (1961)).

31   Adam Piette, 'Between Geological Disposal and Radioactive Time: Beckett, Bowen, Nirex and Onkalo', in eds. Beck and Bishop, *Cold War Legacies: Systems, Theories, Aesthetics* (Edinburgh: EUP, 2016), 103.

32   Philip K. Dick, *The Penultimate Truth* (New York: Belmont, 1964).

33   Piette, 'Between Geological Disposal and Radioactive Time', 102. Something like this had already been seen in Beckett's *Endgame*, a claustrophobic drama in which the blind, old, and damaged wait for death in an empty room much like a generic bunker.

echo on in the twenty-first century home-workplace-bun-ker, shot through with the unifying Wi-Fi signal fixing populations to the universal light of the screen — or for Tanizaki, the house becoming 'penetrated by communication'. In all cases, even within the ideal of the shelter, there is this sense of the light already having entered — populations are required to be unprotected.

This RSG generation of secret government bunkers would be revisisted in dramas of the New Cold War, when they were already quaint or ominous. In Kennedy Martin's *Edge of Darkness*, Detective Craven, the rogue CIA operative Jedburgh, and their ex-miner guide follow a trail of deregulated plutonium via a sumptuous half-forgotten bunker where they relax with vintage wines in an atmosphere of unreality before ploughing on. By this point, protection of the population had itself become a standing joke. In Series 3 of the sitcom *Yes, Minister*, two senior civil servants, looking for a way of distracting MP Jim Hacker with some useless project, hit on fallout shelters, and can hardly contain their mirth:

'Get him to look into civil defence.'

'Civil defence, you mean fallout shelters?'

'Yes, governments long ago decided that civil defence was not a serious issue.'

'Merely a desperate one.'

'And is therefore best left to those whose incompetence can be relied upon.'

'Local authorities.'

Senior civil servant Sir Humphrey persuades Hacker that with current (1982) increased fear, a few more votes might be won by beefing up the shelter programme ('Surely they're just a joke?'); when Hacker presses a council on this, a wide-boy councillor claims that this would mean taking money from school meals and textbooks, but is eventually forced to admit that he already has a shelter place under the Town Hall, and backpedals, though when it turns out that Hacker himself has a place in a shelter, he loses the moral high ground again. The drama of shelter places is comic from start to finish, a succession of manoeuvrings for power with no sense of public interest or even personal survival.

The popular understanding of the absurdity of shelters also gets an outing in an episode of the first series of *Only Fools and Horses* (1981) called 'The Russians Are Coming'. Here, Del Boy comes across some unclaimed lead that Rodney recognises as a nuclear shelter kit, but which he still wants to sell for scrap:

Del: *'What do you suggest we do with it, build it?'*

Rodney: *'This country's just not prepared for war — nobody knows what we're supposed to do in the event.'*

After a dummy run to the allotment where Rodney wants to place the shelter, and some hilarity about trying to move Grandad while tracking the Soviet missiles, some basic arithmetic on air filtering and food supplies shows the brothers that sheltering is pointless. Realising this, they still wonder about their chances of building a post-apocalypse monopoly — 'The end of the world could be just the break we're looking for'. The economic pragmatism behind thermonuclear standoff is laid bare in this kind of silliness: Del Boy is yuppy-ambitious but expendable, he is collateral for the power for which he is trying to summon up some patriotism. At the same time, he recognises along with Jean Baudrillard that 'courage is obsolete' with the government leveraging of automated apocalypse. The rise of an economic rationality over defensibility is further broken down by Jim Hacker later, when he is promoted to PM in the first episode of *Yes, Prime Minister* (1986):

> *General: [The current total warhead number is] not very many — not with 1200 Soviet missiles trained on Britain waiting to retaliate instantly.*
>
> *Prime Minister: Twelve hundred? Still, Britain's always fought against the odds, haven't they? The Armada, the Battle of Britain...*
>
> *Sir Humphrey: Conventional forces are terribly expensive, Prime Minister. Much cheaper just to press a button.*

Influenced by an Austrian-born chief scientific advisor who is 'not one of us', Hacker considers reversing Strath Report wisdom to cancel Trident and reintroduce National Service — though he is quietly blocked by the civil servants who understand what really makes the country work. This is the crux of cheap extinction: a permanent omnicidal threat has become a bureaucratic necessity disguised as public interest; it is economically rational, low-cost and good for morale. This threat has removed the expense of both a serious shelter programme and of armed labour, and set a good example of the efficiency needed in the post-war rebuilding. What Hacker faced was what the '57 White Paper had seen as the foundation of the new Britain: deterrence not defence; halving the number of military personnel; standing down National Service; a shift to automated systems affirming Scarry's deletion of the population.[34] National Service had meant messy human entanglements and demands, even the kind of class consciousness that had to be made obsolete in the postwar technocracy. Correspondingly, some of the strongest expressions of nuclear scepticism came from conventional soldiers who understood the importance of the loss of stakes in fighting — a 2020 paper by former nuclear submariners and Polaris officers, for example, which castigated the spending of 'billions of pounds on deploying and modernising the Trident Nuclear Weapon System'.[35] The population that is unsheltered and 'disarmed', in the Jacobite sense, is the population that improves the condition of the economy, and (following Locke) in supporting the economy really becomes the public.

Thus, the British embrace of the long-ingrained habit of stripping labour and human interference from extinction systems. One of the most iconic expressions of this stripping away of interference comes from the height of the early thermonuclear era: Mordecai Roshwald's *Level 7* (1959), a novel championed by early CND figures including Russell and J.B. Priestley, and later adapted for BBC TV's *Out of the Unknown* series (1966).[36] In Roshwald's story, the behaviour

---

34   Scarry, *Thermonuclear Monarchies*, 43: 'No human beings are needed to carry the weapons on to the battlefield'.

35   Max Channon, 'Ex Royal Navy Commanders question Trident need as coronavirus costs rise', *Plymouth Live*, 2 April 2020: plymouthherald.co.uk/news/uk-world-news/ex-royal-navy-commanders-question-4011611; The Ferret, 'MoD "gagging" its staff from speaking publicly about Trident', *The National*, 3 May 2020: thenational.scot/news/18422680.mod-gagging-staff-speaking-publicly-trident/

36   Mordecai Roshwald, *Level 7* (New York: New American Library, 1959); Wr. Mordecai Roshwald and J.B. Priestley, dir. Rudolph Cartier, *Level 7* (BBC, 1966).

of launch operatives is pared down and shorn of biological response, with lifelong immurement and training that socialises them according to their shelter level (Huxley's *Brave New World* looms large here). One operative's diary records the ensuing war, a morning-long omnicidal exchange between underground 'push-button gods' without embodied response, as the new warriors are told that

> it is not all that important to know exactly what the buttons do, because the orders would be quite explicit: 'Push Button A1', or 'Push Button C2'. It is not certain whether Buttons 4 would actually be used. Some people have said they might prove dangerous even to the country using them.[37]

Operatives are then asked to maintain the abstraction of the conflict as they trigger extinction-level strikes, and see 'a mass of blue and golden points. Aesthetically the picture was quite pleasing... like a continent waiting for an explorer to map it...'. This play of colours is soon finished. Then,

> at 11.21 hours today the 9th of June, I was through with my daily duty. As a matter of fact, I was through with my life's work. I had done my job. My function as PBX Officer was completely fulfilled.
> The loudspeaker said: 'You are free, gentlemen. You may go to your quarters or, if you prefer, stay to watch the results of A4, B4 and C4'.[38]

Crucially, here the erasure of embodied conflict serves an inexorable, progressive logic. The push-button war is 'the ultimate logical form for democracy to take'; the

---

37   Roshwald, *Level 7*, 18.

38   Roshwald, *Level 7*, 96–97, 100.

defeat of barbaric physicality affirms the civilisational form, even as it leads to extinction, as in some sense the operatives had always expected. They are forced to confront this when even the deepest-buried of them run out of life resources and absorb the radioactivity drifting downwards like a dawning realisation, speaking to their opposite numbers through a crackly radio in the last moments and realising that the war arose through the inevitable accident.

The embrace of the certain accident is democratic in its liberating of a population to the condition of extinction-in-waiting and post-human efficiency for which labour-saving is a constant goal. Its sheer efficiency, its ability to spread market rationality throughout a population, is what marks nuclear standoff as the final ascendancy of liberal democracy — which is why, for Winston Churchill, it would soon 'reap its final reward'.[39] The streamlining of launch operatives' behaviour to remove rogue bodily movement also belongs with the technocratic streamlining of workers' behaviour, then evident in the spread of managerial techniques known as time and motion studies. Time and motion studies and the H-bomb are two wings of the same technocratic moment. Both dissolve the body, rationalise all movement, and demand, as one 1957 British Productivity Council (BPC) put it, that workers

Use the simplest and most natural movements possible

Use smooth and even movements

Use symmetrical movements.

---

39   Quoted in Pelopidas, 'The Birth of Nuclear Eternity', 488.

This BPC directive could have been part of the training of the operatives of Roshwald's *Level 7*. Human actors adapt themselves to an extinction assembly line, whose managers are the senior politicians who eventually come to see the removal of their own human response as a statement of fitness to hold office, with commitment to unconditional counter-strike a catechism stated as a condition of public trust. Margaret Thatcher's foreign secretary John Nott, economic liberaliser and cheap extinction advocate, frequently described his own readiness to order a counter-launch on warning. In the early days of the Russia-Ukraine War, the neo-Thatcherite Liz Truss got the applause she needed for her leadership campaign by promising an automation of counter-strike, 'even if it meant global annihilation'.[40] In earlier life, Truss had joined her mother at CND demonstrations, including Faslane marches; in 2015, during his own party leadership, current CND activist Jeremy Corbyn had shown himself to be a fly in the ointment by refusing the catechism, leading to accusations of irresponsibility.[41] Human interference is poison to the nuclear security state that requires constant shows of loyalty. In his own answer to the question of counter-strike, Corbyn was really just remembering the requirement established by the UK's signing of the Nuclear Non-Proliferation Treaty (NPT), 'to pursue negotiations in good faith on effective measures relating to cessation of the nuclear arms race at an early date and to nuclear disarmament' — though Nuclear Weapons States by now commonly ignored this requirement.[42] When

40   Alicia Fitzgerald, 'Liz Truss says she would use nuclear warfare', *Politics*, 24 August 2022: politics.co.uk/news/2022/08/24/truss-nuclear-weapons/

41   BBC News, 'Jeremy Corbyn pressed over whether he'd use nuclear weapons': youtube.com/watch?v=cU-ITKrCr0I

42   Nuclear Non-Proliferation Treaty, Article VI: web.archive.org/

Soviet premier Mikhail Gorbachev refused to automate a counter-strike, leading to the largescale arms reductions agreements of the Reykjavik Accords of 1987, he signalled an unreliability in his own moribund empire. Atlantic leaders can't allow the same.

If the civil defence façade precariously committing the population to cheap extinction — with its *faux* shelters and its deep bureaucratic rationality — was prodded by early CND, Spies for Peace and Roshwald, it would be blown away by Peter Watkins's groundbreaking docudrama *The War Game* (1966). *The War Game* is the kind of research-led intervention that could be drawn on in the 'third nuclear age' of the 2010s onward, mixing drama, documentary, direct-to-camera conversations about real and fictional situations, and voxpops in which people are invited to consider the real cognitive dissonance of current thermonuclear policy. The film begins by pointing out that nuclear forces are increasingly being ranged against conventional forces such that 'the Allies' are preparing to escalate first and force an all-out Soviet counter-attack to avoid their own nukes being wasted. *The War Game* uses expert testimony to track the exchange of bluffs likely to lead to war, and uses this to back a drama describing blast effects a few tens of miles around a one-megaton blast in Rochester. Here the imagery of a home front defence is exploded: firemen look much like the firemen of wartime morale films like Humphrey Jennings's *Fires Were Started* (1943), maintaining morale by describing the endless resilience of British defences (with, as in Watkins, real firemen embedded in the story). However, following the Strath Report's focus on the horror of the firestorm, *The War Game*'s firemen don't put fires out, they are overwhelmed by fire and trapped in poisonous gas to

web/20070807060917/http://www.iaea.org/Publications/Documents/Infcircs/Others/infcirc140.pdf

spend their last minutes being blown around in confusion. In Watkins's film, British cities won't recover — London *Can't* Take It, to adapt the title of a 1940 Jennings film. Revisiting ideologies of endless resilience in the nuclear reality, Watkins defamiliarises Britishness, and its character list of vigilant officials and peaceful householders.

Crucially, *The War Game* is limited neither by the demands of a front-to-back single narrative — realism — nor by the merely fantastic to be written off as doom-mongering. *The War Game* depends on rapid disorienting moves between genres and times, drama, documentary and interview. Nukes are embedded in realist ideologies, but they can't truly command realism, a debate recently played in the 'English New Wave' film that led to kitchen-sink realist cinema: *A Taste of Honey, Saturday Night and Sunday Morning, The Family Way*. *The War Game* is steeped in, and subversive of, any simple consensus realism, using realism against itself to unpack the actual strangeness of the constant extinction barter. The key to undoing nuclear realism is in the unsettling combinations of these modes — characters describing the mass trauma straight to viewers; a GP father confiding about his children's possible leukaemia in a strictly factual mode; compulsory evacuees following real plans to be rejected by their hosts; real figures like the nuclear strategist Herman Kahn being played by actors and describing strategic visions of the war; children rocking with incurable mental illness for which there are no public services; citizens trying to buy sandbags for their own makeshift shelters while the slightly more affluent describe their willingness to shoot their neighbours as encouraged by official civil defence guidelines; family photos mocked up to look blast-damaged while their models' fates are described. Everywhere an odd familiarity hangs over the chaos on social-realist streets. The theatre critic Kenneth Tynan had been more responsible than anyone else for mainstreaming kitchen-sink drama in the mode of John Osborn's *Look Back in Anger*; he would become one of *The War Game*'s great defenders through its controversies. *The War Game* brings out what was implicit in that consensus familiarity.

A warping of social realism then becomes a way for that enthusiastic watcher of *The War Game*, Mick Jackson, to conceive the officially unthinkable, which he would do in *Threads*. The cognitive dissonance is so powerful that governments don't even have to hide information, they merely have to disincentivise concentrating on it. In the days before the war, the military go door to door to distribute a leaflet on civil defence (or the lack of civil defence that leaves householders to themselves) — but why, asks the documentary-maker-character within the drama, was this information not distributed earlier? In answering, the soldier reverts to the historical fact that civil defence has always been kept slightly beyond the level of consciousness that would allow it a democratic function:

> *'Well, a copy was prepared some years ago, but it didn't sell very well.'*

> *'It wasn't free?'*

> *'Oh no, no. It cost ninepence.'*

In contrast to the familiar story about *Threads*, *The War Game*'s alt-realism *didn't* traumatise a generation, since it was refused by the BBC who had commissioned it — it was suppressed, as Watkins himself puts it. Julie McDowall describes this quiet censorship nicely: the official reason was that the film would be too horrifying for mass consumption, but this meant 'subtly blaming the British public, who would be unable to tell fact from fiction; too ignorant to realise this was not a true documentary, and too lazy to put the kids to bed'.[43] Watkins reports that he was warned that broadcast would risk twenty thousand suicides — oddly echoing the moral panic at the end of the Meiji era, when Japan's status as a British satellite was threatened by ritual suicides following the emperor's own death, the vaguely Jacobite-sounding re-physicalisation of conflict.[44] The film did have a run at the National Film Theatre, and, less familiarly, it won an Academy Award (Best Documentary feature, 1967), mortifying the BBC and prompting Watkins to ask his friend Elizabeth Taylor to get hold of the statue after the ceremony.[45]

The War Game remains the great statement of shelter dissonance and the addictiveness of cheap extinction. It is telling that Watkins's breakthrough had come with *Culloden* (1964), notable for the kind of generic experimentation — non-actors standing for actors, war drama done as reportage — that would soon be turned to nuclear apocalypse. The choice of the Battle of *Culloden* allows the film to directly revisit the vanquishing of the Highland clan system and the unification of the the new Britain under an ideal of abstracted violence. After *The War Game*, Watkins would extend the critique into a series of anti-war and anti-nuke films, including *Gladiators* (1969 — small groups of draftees play out a proxy war on reality TV to prevent real-world war), *Punishment Park* (1971 — protestors are left in the California desert to be hunted by the National Guard), *Fällan/The Trap* (1975 — a conflict between totalitarian superpowers sees the family of a Swedish government worker celebrate New Year in a nuclear shelter), and the monumental *Resan* (1987 — fourteen and a half hours of docudrama

---

43   McDowall, *Attack Warning Red!*, 193.

44   McDowall, *Attack Warning Red!*, 194.

45   McDowall, *Attack Warning Red!*, 197.

on government plans for, and public awareness of, nuclear arsenals around the world). Watkins would also expand on the mobility between genres put to such troubling use in the alt-realism of the Rochester blast, a mobility he sees as a necessary defence against a permanent security naturalised by what he calls, in *Notes on the Media Crisis* (2010), a media 'monoform' dictating a homogeneity of expression. The banning of *The War Game*, Watkins says, showed 'the standardisation of the audiovisual form resulting in the creation of an increasingly hierarchical and manipulative relationship with the audience (the public)', and through this formal foreclosure the working class are reduced to 'populist programmes... [to] identify with the characters, and with the "everyday" plots and issues involved'.[46] The generic disturbance of *The War Game* or *Resan*, then, is a way of breaking through the warped patriotism of cheap extinction. It leaves the challenge of how to think about nuclear civil defence dissonance today — rather than letting the prone population sink into Cold War nostalgia.

Something like the Watkins role would be taken up by figures like Duncan Campbell, investigative journalist and perpetual irritant to Tory governments, who highlighted really existing emergency plans including banning domestic travel to keep populations static.[47] By now, the comedy of the civil defence façade had faded (the Civil Defence Corps was stood down in 1968) and been replaced by dark visions of individual imprisonment. Most familiarly, the late 1970s *Protect and Survive*, an exercise in cognitive dissonance that looked

---

46   Peter Watkins, *Notes on the Media Crisis* (Barcelona: Museu D'Art Contemporani de Barcelona, 2010).
47   Heuser, *Nuclear Mentalities*, 19; Duncan Campbell, *War Plan UK: The Truth About Civil Defence in Britain* (London: Burnett, 1982).

like a traumatising extension of '70s public information films. *Protect and Survive*'s melodic minor thirds, chunky animations and cold-comfort narration of Patrick Allen (on his way to collaboration with Vic Reeves and Bob Mortimer) accidentally make the coming of the cold, blind millennia look like kids' TV, turning the cartoon itself into perhaps the most iconic work of accidental analogue horror ever made.

By now, with the proliferation of intercontinental ballistic missiles, government bunkers were dispensed with, and the confusion of evacuations shown by Watkins settled into a policy of 'shelter in place' — the official advice was not to move, a kind of apotheosis of the individuating role of nukes. The pre-blast scenes of *Threads* describe plans preventing citizens from moving to safer parts of the country, communicated by a police officer who turns back a family car trying to escape Sheffield: 'If I were you I'd do home and sit tight, that's what they're advising people to do'. Staying put had always been part of the calculations behind the strategic bargaining that kept Mutually Assured Destruction in place — populations *have to* be prone to make the arithmetic of nuclear deterrent work.

'Shelter in place' shows, as Campbell says, that what is protected by nuclear civil defence is not the population but the sheer managerial power that is always the real core of nuclear authority (civil defence 'has, as its primary objective, the preservation of government — if need be, against the civil population').[48] *Protect and Survive* was only released after it was leaked by nuclear consciousness-raisers, and, as with *The War Game*, its civil defence pamphlets had a cover price so that reading was disincentivised. *Protect and Survive* was in turn seized on by the wave of new docudramas I have called Nuclear Gothic: often prime TV depictions of

---

48   Campbell, *War Plan UK*, 15.

the great dissonances, as in the Jeremy Paxman–narrated 1980 *Panorama* that exposed it, the *TV Eye* 'Target Britain' (1980), or the 1982 *QED* Jackson used as a spotter for *Threads*. All showed that *Protect and Survive* was so individualistic that, in fact, it made little sense; survival depended on an unfeasible degree of self-reliance (stock your larder, treat your family and bury your dead, become an expert in DIY and chemistry), a house large enough to undertake the necessary conversions, and a disregarding of complex dependencies. People were free agents, but they had already been bartered; they were entrepreneurs of their own survival, but with no conception of an infrastructure making survival possible. *Protect and Survive* has long since become the stuff of memes, though the directors of these exposés might have preferred if they prompted consideration of current plans: the way populations are still expected to remain prone, the learned helplessness that keeps nuclear war preparations just under the level of everyday attention. The 2004 Civil Contingencies Act affirms the need to maintain the continuity of government at all costs, with 'shelter in place' for the bartered population; movement is still restricted, and roads will likely be blocked. The Resilience Framework of 2022 barely mentions nuclear emergency, and suggests that civil defence has been made even more pointless by hypersonic missiles. Police now have vastly increased surveillance powers, besides which, putative refugees will easily be picked up in railway stations while trying to change their password to get into the app to look for information about non-existent trains.

Meanwhile, since the constant promise of extinction would now be part of the democratic bargain, its interruption, in CND agitation and similar, would increasingly have to be seen as treasonous. The wave of nuclear-sceptical folk politics that characterised the late 1950s was countered by mass-market stories that the communist dystopia nuclear consciousness-raisers would bring. In Constantine FitzGibbon's *When the Kissing Had to Stop* (1960; ITV series 1962), peacenik factions are allowed into power by a Labour government that soon falls to Soviet collusion. In John le Carré's *The Spy Who Came In from the Cold* (film 1965; book 1963), Claire Bloom's naive librarian is drawn by Richard Burton's hard-bitten alcoholic spy into a world of East German intrigue where she realises her folly. The counter-imagination was persistent, and often misguided — some early CND activists were Soviet sympathisers (Michael Randle had helped a Soviet double-agent escape from Wormwood Scrubs); most weren't. The staple thinking of 1950s CND was non-alignment. J.B. Priestly, who had railed against Nye Bevan's support for H-bombs, was anti-communist, as were the Direct Action Committee, the CND group responsible for radical protests trying to increase understanding of nuclear weapons.[49] In any case, CND-type sceptics, whether due to naivety (like le Carré's Liz Gold) or too much lower-middle-class access to higher education, were seen as threatening an organic British gentleness. Through the infiltration narrative, moral discussion of nuclear weapons could be countered with, as Drew Milne puts it, 'accusations of offering naive or conspiratorial support for Soviet communism, despite the fact that it was the United States that pioneered and used atomic weapons'.[50]

Nuclear weapons, in this ideology, are always defensive and unwillingly accepted by peaceful representative forces; they're always urgent at any given moment; and they always do deter, even if International Relations scholars describe them as a liability. But the dramas of the first two nuclear eras make the story of population protection

---

49   Taylor, *Against the Bomb*, 181, 151.

50   Drew Milne, 'Poetry After Hiroshima?: Notes on Nuclear Implicature', *Angelaki* 22-3, 87–102: 94.

through official non-aggression much harder to believe.[51] In the third (post-2010s) nuclear era, nukes are again casually linked to national strength and even economic growth. They protect a way of life, and they are an investment against uncertainty. Of course, although nukes have a fundamental place in the formal economy, and in a sense set the ground on which the formal economy can exist, they're not really cheap in any way meaningful for the populations they're supposed to protect. In March 2024, after a decade of economic stagnation, a House of Commons report noted an MoD overspend of £17 billion on a ten-year defence plan even after its initial increase to £46.3 billion.[52] Cheap extinction is a kind of economic reflex, a set of short-term fixes that trail an eternity behind them. This spending *prevents* prosperity, someone like E.P. Thompson would have argued; but it is projected onto 'the nation' as a general good, and deeply entangled with a British form of welfare. It needs a Watkins-like imagination to disentangle it.

---

51   Freedman, *Britain and Nuclear Weapons*, 140; Cortright and Väyrynen, *Towards Nuclear Zero*, 97.
52   House of Commons, MoD Equipment Plan, 2023–2033: committees.parliament.uk/publications/43732/documents/216970/ default/. In the US, estimates from the Congressional Budget Office, Nuclear Threat Initiative, and the Ploughshares Fund suggest a total bill from 1940 to 2024 that may be around $12 trillion.

NUKES AS FEEDBACK

For the radicals coalescing around new Conservative leader
Margaret Thatcher after 1975, gathering around thinktanks
like the Institute of Economic Affairs (IEA) and plotting
the coming order, the relative quiet following recent nuclear accords (the Treaty on the Non-Proliferation of Nuclear
Weapons, the Strategic Arms Limitation Talks Agreement
I) hid terrible dangers. Warsaw Pact countries were looking
for infiltration opportunities, increasing their continental
nuclear forces, and smelling blood in a weakened Atlantic
capitalism. For Thatcherites, the communist threat was both
geopolitical and domestic, seen in both the medium-range
SS20s rumbling across Central Europe and the erosion of
individual property through the debauching of the currency
by communist trade unions.[1] The failure to observe natural
law, the conversion of everything to the evaluable, put these
infiltrators, like the Japanese had been before them, beneath moral capability. It put them, as some establishment
neo-Lockeans explicitly said, beneath the acceptable limit of
the human, so that there were no limits to the violence that
could be levied against them.[2] If some economic libertarians

---

1   Margaret Thatcher, 'The Ideals of an Open Society', in Bow
Group, *The Right Angle: Three Studies in Conservatism* (London:
Bow, 1978), 3–10: 5–6.
2   Robert Moss, 'Freedom and Subversion', in Ed. Rhodes
Boyson, *1985: An Escape from Orwell's 1984* (Enfield: Churchill
Press, 1975), 107–21.

had high-minded ideas of non-aggression, the anti-communism of working politicians in this movement underwrote an extraordinarily uniform commitment to renewed nuclear deterrence. Nuclear deterrence was crucial to countering the communist erosion of values. And in fact the sale of the new Trident nuclear weapons system was completed against the backdrop of the urban riots often ascribed to Geoffrey Howe's fiscal-disciplining '81 budget. Uniformity on the need for nuclear deterrence was one of the founding conditions of the neoliberal condition.

But as tempting as it is to attribute this terminal naturalisation of nuclear arsenals to Thatcher's governments, Trident univocality goes back to the acceptance of the money-discipline coming with the IMF bailout of 1976. The bailout required the abandoning of inflationary policies by the Labour government (PM James Callaghan's famous 'That option no longer exists') — and assurances of Atlantic nuclear security to Americans looking for a European bulwark against Soviet force.[3] Transatlantic trade relations had long been tied to nuclear assurances; in 1958 British H-bomb production had helped affirm Anglo-American links, and the '70s conditions are worth remembering for how they bracketed nukes together with a need for a rationalised, stripped-down labour force. Declassified transcripts of conversations with President Ford show Callaghan leveraging the spectre of nuclear weakness to try to ensure US-led financial help.[4] Nuclear disarmament was the other option that no longer existed.

---

3   Freedman, *Britain and Nuclear Weapons*, 85; Stoddart, *Facing Down the Soviet Union*, 174, 5.

4   Stoddart, *Facing Down the Soviet Union*, 18; *The Standard*, 'Callaghan threatened to scrap nuclear weapons', 12 April 2012: standard.co.uk/hp/front/callaghan-threatened-to-scrap-nuclear-weapons-7278160.html

In this, Callaghan took the opposite path to the fiction-al PM Harry Perkins in Chris Mullin's speculative novel of a non-aligned Labour government, *A Very British Coup* (1982). Callaghan reaffirmed nuclear alignment with the US; Perkins presses ahead with disarmament despite pres-sure from the press, the civil service and American money, and explores international relationships not subservient to superpowers. Callaghan's turn to nuclear realism even marked a crescendo in his struggle with domestic trade unions: at the January '79 peak of the battle known as the Winter of Discontent came his meeting with President Carter in Guadeloupe.[5] It was the sense that Britain was regaining its geopolitical pride *as a nuclear power* that gave Callaghan his cheery demeanour on returning from Guade-loupe, an image made iconic by the tabloid journalists who put it together with binbags left uncollected by striking workers and the misquotation: 'Crisis? What Crisis?'[6] If a transcendental mode of violence was in hand, the longer battle to restabilise money would also be won.

The culture of the nuclear deterrent and that of un-bound capital are both cultures of untrammeled positive feedback. Both demand — as described in Roshwald or in early stories of human cybernetics — the removal of any blocks to automated progress. Nuclear weapons' battle is cybernetic battle, a sublimation of fighting to the purely automated — and what characterised the new Tory rev-olution that would eternalise nukes is that cybernetics would be made explicitly virtuous. Thus John Hoskyns and Norman Strauss's influential policy strategy document *Stepping Stones* (1977) — a pamphlet left, as legend has it,

---

5   Stoddart, *Facing Down the Soviet Union*, 2, 70, 125.

6   Turner, *Britain's International Role*, 115–24; Stoddart, *Facing Down the Soviet Union*, 2–4, 215; Peter Malone, *The British Nuclear Deterrent* (London: Croom Helm, 1984), 37, 41.

under the seats of every delegate at Tory conference, and proselytising a world of uninterrupted positive feedback. For *Stepping Stones*, as for many IEA thinkers, moral sickness results from a rejection of 'simple arithmetic', and can be cured through a systematic streamlining-away of human interference. Here flow charts identify the catastrophic blocks to the healthy circulation of money, allowing them to be removed — especially, Hoskyns and Strauss think, by the disciplining of unions.[7] Voting is a market choice, the citizen is a consumer, and political decisions should be made according to the Newtonian laws. And following Friedrich Hayek's *The Constitution of Liberty* (1960), deviations from the self-evolving *telos* of market rationality (blocks to positive feedback) enable tyrannical politicians and should be prevented by any means.[8]

The nuclear overcoming of politics in fact goes right back to H.G. Wells's foundational dystopia/utopia *The World Set Free*, in which, after coming to terms with the post-apocalypse condition of permanent deterrence, emerging elites feel that 'it is doubtful if we shall ever see again a phase of human existence in which "politics", that is to say a partisan interference with the ruling sanities of the world, will be the dominant interest among serious men'.[9] In the new

---

7   John Hoskyns, Norman S. Strauss et al, *Stepping Stones*, London, self-published, 1977, especially appendix diagrams: cps. org.uk/wp-content/uploads/2021/07/111026104730-5B6518B-5823043FE9D7C54846CC7FE31.pdf

8   John Beck and Ryan Bishop, 'Introduction' to Beck and Bishop *Cold War Legacies: Systems, Theories, Aesthetics* (Edinburgh: EUP, 2016), 17.

9   H.G. Wells, *The World Set Free*, 85: ia801605.us.archive.org/ view_archive.php?archive=/33/items/GutenbergENzip/43.zip&-file=World%20Set%20Free%2C%20The%20-%20H.%20G.%20 Wells%2C%202006%20%28110p%29.pdf

Tory version of this, the evisceration of politics needs a new reverence for feedback loops — an unlimited feedback explosion, or as Paul Virilio described the role of nukes in *War and Cinema* (1984), an 'assumption of cybernetics into the heavens'.[10] For Hayek, cybernetics was a new form of Adam Smith's invisible hand, a divine market power guiding progress.[11] The cleansing of money would require what IEA writers saw as a permanent chain reaction — the auto-abstraction of violence, or the total deregulation of markets that would come to be known as the Big Bang.[12]

With the nuclear version of the big bang, the permanent species-eclipsing explosion, nukes would not be something to be chosen in the future, they would be immanent and explode constantly. Virilio again — it is 'not so much that [the bomb] will explode, but that it exists and is exploding in our own minds'.[13] The endless explosion guarantees the permacrisis, naturalised competition containing locked-in extinction, a new permanence seen in Thatcher's own commitment to 'dynamic stalemate'.[14] If the new economics depended on the idea that there was no alternative,

---

10   Paul Virilio, trans. Patrick Camiller, *War and Cinema: The Logistics of Perception* (London: Verso, 1989 (1984)), 2, 7.

11   F.A. Hayek, *Law, Legislation and Liberty* (London: Routledge, 2012 (1973)).

12   Pete Dorey, 'The "Stepping Stones" Programme: The Conservative Party's Struggle to Develop a Trade-Union Policy, 1975–79', *Historical Studies in International Relations* 35, July 2014, 89–116: 89–90, 103, 114.

13   Paul Virilio, trans. Mark Polizzotti, *Speed and Politics: An Essay on Dromology* (New York: Semiotext(e), 1986 (1977)), 150.

14   Ruston, *A Say in the End of the World*, 31. Thatcher herself was resigned to the fact that nuclear weapons would be used someday, and, along with her advisor, senior civil servant Michael Quinlan, was sure that they were irreversible.

no permissible deviation from the singular progress, the new thermonuclear realism depended on what the short-lived field of Nuclear Criticism called 'nuclearism': neutral-sounding terminologies making nukes seem apolitical and 'devoid of any ideological concerns'.[15] Total violence has to be constantly leveraged, and the leveraging tends to become unspoken, part of the everyday language of interaction. As William Cahloupka asks of the many distractions of the post–Cold War era, 'Could it be that we have been talking about nukes constantly?'[16] The task of the nuclear imagination, then, is to denaturalise, showing how the constant explosion is still based on contingent desires.

Positive feedback then gets inserted into everyday life and immerses relationships in the solvent of value, standing in for communication in an exhausted culture driven by an extinction unconscious. If this is the goal of *Stepping Stones*, it appeared against the background of an energetic argument about what feedback loops were doing to humans and environment. For the ecology movement appearing in the early '70s, untrammeled positive feedback was already evident in an environmental nihilism seen in explosive population growth, pollution, and soil degradation. Positive-feedback degradation was described by the Club of Rome's *The Limits to Growth*, by Ernst Schumacher's *Small is Beautiful*, by the often neo-tribalist and sometimes esoteric arguments of the *Ecologist* magazine, and by the Coventry-based founders of PEOPLE, a group, formed to warn about exponential pollution, that would gradually morph into the Green Party. In the nuclear field, cybernetics also began to give rise to a horror of the 'hyperobject', particularly plutonium, an artificial substance that, once awak-

---

15   Heuser, *Nuclear Mentalities?*, 53.

16   William Chaloupka, *Knowing Nukes: The Politics and Culture of the Atom* (Minneapolis: University of Minnesota Press, 1992), 17.

ened, seemed to have a (half-)life of its own.[17] In Stephen Poliakoff's 1977 contribution to the *Play for Today* series, *Stronger than the Sun*, a worker in a Magnox reactor becomes fascinated by the sample she has smuggled out, only to find the press uninterested. She is more and more drawn to the strange agency of the hyperobject, feeling herself entangled with it, and lets it take her down.[18] In Kennedy Martin's *Edge of Darkness*, the American entrepreneur Grogan gets carried away with his speech on the expansive future of plutonium, with its indefinite reach across the cosmos, but misses its embodied effects, his speech punctuated by terminal coughing. For numerous nuclear commentators, radiation marks the return of the repressed, the out-of-mind that sweeps away human plans.

The open-ended nuclear explosion is the arch-symbol of positive feedback. The permanent explosion 'opens' the future, as classical liberalism understands it, but it begins to close the door for intelligent species — as Craven's environmental activist daughter, Emma, tries to explain in *Edge of Darkness*. Leading a security organisation backed by British intelligence and responsible for Emma's death, Grogan is welded to the plutonium drive towards perpetual expansion, now revealed as ownership-towards-extinction. American ownership-towards-extinction remains the overarching sign of the radionuclide era: when J.D. Vance visited Greenland in March 2025 to unload the kind of gaslighting only found in post-truth environments marked by exhausted attention, he was following an earlier precedent of Cold War Denmark being secretly given permission to American

---

17   This term is probably most familiar from Timothy Morton, *Hyperobjects: Philosophy and Ecology after the End of the World* (Minneapolis: University of Minnesota Press, 2014).

18   Wr. Stephen Poliakoff, dir. Michael Apted, *Stronger Than the Sun*, BBC, 1977.

forces to build a military base in Thule/Pituffik, contravening Denmark's nuclear-free policy — and in 1969, Thule
had been the site of a crash involving a nuclear-armed B52
bomber that left a spill of jet fuel containing Plutonium isotopes with half-lives of up to twenty-four thousand years.
Plutonium marks ownership-towards-extinction, spilled
across the ice in perpetuity.

The nuclear orientation of cybernetics, weapons systems' eclipse of biological intention, had even been a cultural theme in the decade before *Stepping Stones*. The classic
Fail Safe (1964; novel 1962) describes bombers becoming
effectively autonomous, escaping leaders' intentions and
leaving them scrambling to broker an exchange of population megadeaths to try to limit the damage — the US
President's bombing of New York leading to the iconic
dead phone line that ends the film. In Stanley Kubrick's
Doctor Strangelove (1964), comic archetypes blunder into
an omnicidal destruction compelled by automations they
can't understand. Dramas of the cybernetic weapon system
are clear on this: human actors are already adjuncts to autonomous security systems. Kubrick's dark comedy partly
derives from the players acting as if there are still real fights
being fought — Peter Sellers's Group Captain Mandrake,
left with a gammy leg and emotional trauma by the last war,
or Slim Pickens's Major Kong, the cowboy who describes
nuclear combat as 'toe to toe'. This soldiering is already
irrelevant to the cybernetics of progress. In the war against
sticky human desires, the removal of decision-making itself
increasingly disappears from view, as in the virtuous promise to launch, from Roshwald's PBX Officer to Liz Truss.
By the Thatcher-Reagan era, the US had adopted Launch
on Warning; by 1985, the Soviets had adopted the Dead
Hand system (Perimeter), which guaranteed a retaliation

strike after everyone had been killed.[19] This acceleration past human reaction was accompanied by a push towards limitless yields — Leo Szilard's hypothesised cobalt bomb, for example, a 'salted' nuke producing massively increased amounts of radioactive material and rendering the earth uninhabitable; or the extinction weapon the generals of *Doctor Strangelove* can only describe in terms of competition as usual — 'We must not allow a Doomsday Machine gap!'

Untrammeled feedback, meanwhile, multiplies miscommunications between superpowers, laying nuclear standoff open to the Babel written into the Enlightenment desire for a 'universal [English] language'. In the New Cold War, Moscow's notoriously dysfunctional intelligence operation Raketno-Yadernoe Napadenie (RYaN) rewarded operatives who claimed to have found positive-feedback signs that NATO might be readying to attack (lights on late in Whitehall, market movements in the price of medical supplies...), while ignoring any negative feedback that might have suggested normalcy, over-interpreting random movements and nearly causing an all-out response to NATO's exercise Able Archer 83. Soviet defencelessness against feedback loops of paranoia in their own bureaucracy was the basis of a number of nuclear war stories. In Robert Stone's 1998 alternate-history film *World War III*, a hardliner who comes to power instead of Mikhail Gorbachev struggles to avoid state collapse and is pressed into a single nuclear strike that inevitably causes escalation. Meanwhile NATO intelligence was, and is, often puzzled by Soviet/Russian unwillingness to think like rational market individuals (their 'mystical' thinking). In the New Cold War, the Soviets had the cold

---

19   Eugene Burdick and Harvey Wheeler, *Fail-Safe* (New York: McGraw Hill, 1962); Franklin, *War Stars*, 207. Post-Soviet Russia has retained some form of Perimeter — how effective it is we don't know, as is typical for nuclear posture.

Martian intellect of classic science fiction, representing the inhumanity beyond the market — the invaders of H.G. Wells's *War of the Worlds* (1898) morphing into the invaders of the hammy film *Red Dawn* (1984), in which Western European weakness somehow triggers a Soviet invasion of the American mainland.[20] The collapse of the nuclear Soviet empire was scary enough; it needs to be updated, of course, for an imploding nuclear Atlantic empire, or as Drew Milne and John Kinsella put this, 'The risks of a collapsing capitalist system taking the world down with it are clear'.[21]

The submission to nuclear cyber-capital, though, also gave rise to the last great wave of nuclear-sceptical culture before the terminal nuclear realism of the millennium. E.P. Thompson agrees with Hayek that the nuclear condition makes the political impossible — though for Thompson, of course, this is the problem, not the goal.[22] Nuclear standoff, for Thompson, belongs to a moment when the profit motive has slipped any imperative of productivity or utility. Exterminism is a terminal phase characterised by autonomous development; it is Virilio's ascent of cybernetics to the heavens. What, he asks, does this imply for a 'correspondent social system — a distinct organisation of labour, research and operation... a distinctive organisation of production supported by many state-adjacent groups...[23] Or 'if "the hand-mill gives you society with the feudal lord;

---

20   Mary Midgley, 'Deterrence, Provocation and the Martian Temperament', in ed. Fred Holroyd, *Thinking About Nuclear Weapons: Analyses and Prescriptions* (Beckenham, Kent: Croom Helm, 1985), 73–90; Ruston, *A Say in the End of the World*, 188.

21   John Kinsella and Drew Milne, 'Nuclear Theory Degree Zero', in eds. Kinsella and Milne, *Nuclear Theory Degree Zero: Essays Against the Nuclear Android* (Abingdon: Routledge, 2021), 8.

22   Thompson, 'Notes on Exterminism', 8.

23   Thompson, 'Notes on Exterminism', 4.

the steam-mill, society with the industrial capitalist", what are we given by those Satanic mills which are now at work, grinding out the means of human extermination?'[24]

The answer to Thompson's question — still too seldom asked at a time when the permacrisis makes nuclear rearmament look like a necessary defence measure beyond all political question — has something to do with the insertion of evaluation into each step of interaction, the sublimation of conflict to value at all points. Once a state has allowed its economy to be taken for absolute securitisation, Thompson says, politics becomes purely reactive and 'the ruling groups come to need perpetual war crisis, to legitimate their rule... and to divert attention from the manifest irrationality of the operation'.[25] At this moment of hardening, actions come from 'bureaucratic decisions rather than out of the play of market forces' — the jargon of liberation becomes dependent on feedback systems, societies move into algorithmic fascism, and weapons 'seem to grow of their own accord'.[26] Such weapons then come to 'threaten the very empires of [their] origin'.[27] Nukes now act in terms of 'an autonomous self-generating thrust'.[28] They take on their own agency and break through any human intentions towards conflict, such that, as Virilio says, 'if ancient weapons deterred us from interrupting movement, the new weapons deter us from interrupting the arms race'.[29]

One touchstone for Thompson's argument here is Marx's early grappling in the section of the *Grundrisse* known as the 'Fragment on Machines', a text whose rise in popularity in

---

24 Thompson, 'Notes on Exterminism', 4–5.

25 Thompson, 'Notes on Exterminism', 18, 19, 22.

26 Thompson, 'Notes on Exterminism', 5.

27 Thompson, 'Notes on Exterminism', 21.

28 Thompson, 'Notes on Exterminism', 20, 21.

29 Virilio, *Speed and Politics*, 147.

the new millennium would parallel 'No Future' critiques of neoliberalism and mark the extinction unconscious even as nuclear arsenals themselves seemed to dip beneath the level of attention. According to the 'Fragment on Machines',

> the means of labour passes through different metamorphoses, whose culmination is the *machine*, or rather, an *automatic system of machinery*... set in motion by an automaton, a moving power that moves itself; this automaton consisting of numerous mechanical and intellectual organs, so that the workers themselves are cast merely as its conscious linkages.[30]

The feedback explosion, stripping away everything outside of rational economic decision, leaves the flat-affect 'conscious linkages' described in Roshwald's *Level 7* or seen in the Thatcherite lust for counter-launch. This is the rise of the civilised sociopath, corresponding to a post-industrial economy in which nothing physical is produced and human response is fuel for competition. The naturalisation of nukes brings the era of cybernetic empathy. The era of bureaucratically ingrained automation has been marked by this civilised sociopathy. It makes relationships performative, while it demands the sublimation of actual violence. The negotiation of meaning is progressively converted to feedback, and feedback becomes compulsory, even a condition of survival. Even the most socially minded organisations now issue automated requests for feedback, reducing

---

30   Karl Marx, 'Fragment on Machines;, from *Grundrisse* (1857-1861): archive.org/stream/TheFragmentOnMachinesKarlMarx/The%20_Fragment%20on%20Machines_%20-%20Karl%20 Marx_djvu.txt; also discussed in Ryan Bishop, 'Smart Dust and Remote Sensing: The Political Subject in Autonomous Systems', in eds. Beck and Bishop, *Cold War Legacies,* 273–88.

response to number as a condition of 'improvement'. The feedback bomb increasingly and virtuously squeezes out any space for shared meaning or action. Feedback is realist, as far as company survival goes. It is normal, but it is also an extinction pathway.

The nuclear condition, then, should be seen as the normal accompaniment of the positive-feedback explosion. The positive feedback loop that strips away labour costs also demands the indefinite sublimation of violence, to the point of extinction. Still, twenty-first century revivals of ideas of positive feedback — the many tails of accelerationism, left and right, and campaigns to overcome the entropic politics that characterised late neoliberalism — have tended to be quiet about that feedback's anchor in the extinction-bound weapon. A Deleuzo-Guattarian recuperation of the feedback loop has been a recurring theme in the twenty-first century, sometimes seen as the source of a revolutionary escape from the hell of the same.[31] One likely source for this is the 'War Machine' section of Deleuze and Guattari's *A Thousand Plateaus*, in which the always-deterritorialising war machine points in the opposite direction to the state's disciplinary urge, resisting the state's tendency to return revolutionary desire to hierarchical or 'striated' space.[32] Deleuze and Guattari's war machine works through feedback-intensification of energies that slip regulation. A problem emerges, though, in the conversion of Deleuzo-Guattarian feedback for the Lockean government of the Anglosphere, now renaturalised by Thatcherism — for

---

31   E.g. Acid Horizon, *Anti-Oculus: A Philosophy of Escape* (London: Repeater, 2024). The phrase 'hell of the same' is associated with Jean Baudrillard's *La transparence du mal/ The transparency of evil* (London: Verso, 1993 (1990)).

32   Gilles Deleuze and Félix Guattari, *A Thousand Plateaus* (London: Bloomsbury, 2013 (1980)).

which market freedoms are always already the form of state power. With the 'reterritorialising' of the Big Bang, the radical deregulation of financial markets in the eighties, came a much more banal Brit nationalism, with its commitment to the deep state and absolute security; not a *Blade Runner* wild west, but the eternal same of the unwritten constitution. For libertarian advocates of endless nuclear proliferation, proliferation means more security, but only if all nuclear powers behave exactly according to the market rationality expected by Anglo-American natural law; that is, only if there are never any accidents, brain farts or rogue actors.[33]

As John Beck and Ryan Bishop describe, 'systems thinking' (or flowchart systems analysis, or cybernetics) is double-edged, both a securitisation and an emancipation.[34] Before the generation of Elon Musk gave effective accelerationism a bad name, some version of a machine-allied escape from entropy was promoted by the nuclear disarmament scientists whose work made them unusually attuned to species lifespans — nuclear pile pioneer Leo Szilard, for example; or Carl Sagan, popular astronomer, disarmament campaigner, and contributor to SETI, who argued for the establishment of an interplanetary presence in terms of an everyday ethics. At the same time, accelerationism's own nuclear undercurrent has tended to be overlooked amid the glyphs and cyborgs. One of Nick Land's key images

---

33   Bertrand Lemennicier, 'Nuclear Weapons: Proliferation or Monopoly?', in ed. Hans-Hermann Hoppe, *The Myth of National Defence: Essays on the Theory and History of Security Production* (Auburn AL: Ludwig von Mises Institute, 2003), 127–43. 'It is important to liberalize the right to have extremely dangerous weapons and accept their dissemination among nations or individuals' (138).
34   Beck and Bishop, 'Introduction' to Beck and Bishop *Cold War Legacies*, 9.

for modernity, placed more or less at the English scientific revolution, has been an overwhelming of the *control rods* of tradition, leaving a self-evolving explosion.[35] But the kind of philosophical entrepreneurialism that gave rise to early accelerationism tends to imagine an apocalypse perceived as the warm dissolution of the human into silicon familiar from cyberpunk, rather than the cold dark millennia promised by constant nuclear threat.

Maybe this tendency is to be expected of a line of thought intellectually anchored in the late 1990s, a moment of peak *heiwaboke* (cultural habit shaped by the expectation of peace). But if the early accelerationist moment did belong within neoliberal realism, then naturalised nukes belong to the 'No Future' condition most familiar from Mark Fisher. The story widely told in the 2000s and 2010s of how neoliberalism arrested time is at heart the story of the arrest of politics by the abstraction of all violence under the unreachable positive loop, the present progressively overtaken by like retro, the past sifted for value. The collapse of the *difference* of the past, the ability of other times to mark something other than a streamlined extension of an empty present, creates an extinction feeling, a learned helplessness, even an embrace of extinction and its tools as homely. Naturalised nukes are at the heart of this frozen alienation. In the decade or so following *Stepping Stones*, this alienation was even given its own name: 'nuclear madness'. Nuclear madness is still a feature of everyday Atlantic life, though now commonly repressed or displaced onto more everyday forms of dysphoria. But during the New Cold War, nuclear madness was such a cultural staple that it should probably be one

---

35   Alexander Galloway and Benjamin Noys, 'Crash and Burn: Debating Accelerationism', *3am Magazine*, Oct-Nov 2014: 3am-magazine.com/3am/crash-and-burn-debating-accelerationism/

of the go-to library images for '80s documentaries, along-side shoulder pads and wine bars.

Nuclear madness isn't like regular horror, because it is a compulsory expectation. It is part of how the weapon works on populations, and it is as old as the nuclear era. Even five years before the Trinity tests, in a short story called 'Blowups Happen', nuclear madness was imagined by the hard-science-fiction writer Robert Heinlein. Heinlein's early marker sets the nuclear madness in an Arizona fission reactor running in a sub-critical state but ready at any moment to tip over into uncontrolled feedback. Its workers are forced to live with the constant threat of an uncontrollable explosion that could 'conceivably destroy the entire human race', an atmosphere that produces an everyday grind of psychosis and exhaustion and leaves operatives, managers and psychiatrists constantly observing one another for signs of the 'blow-up'.[36] Heinlein himself cycled through a set of beliefs we might today liken to Hayekian libertarianism, Wellsian world government, and Land-like right-accelerationism, and was later read by the sci-fi fan Ronald Reagan, eventually joining Reagan's government as a speechwriter creating speeches on the US's proposed Strategic Defence Initiative/'Star Wars' shield (one of the key elements in the terrifying mid-1980s destabilisation). The best-known trigger for Reagan's nuclear position, though, was *The Day After* (1983), an American *Threads* equivalent that was notoriously sanitised compared to the Sheffield drama, but effective enough to make the president reach out to Soviet premier Gorbachev.

Reagan's epiphany text, *The Day After*, was a typical product of the year that saw a peak of both the feedback-cleans-

---

36   Robert Heinlein, 'Blowups Happen', *Astounding*, 1940: baen. com/Chapters/0743471598/0743471598___4.htm., n.p.

ing of money and nuclear madness. In 1983, James Thompson noted extraordinary levels of trauma among the young in particular — with more than half of teenagers sure that nuclear war would occur in their lifetimes — and a 'disaster syndrome' that would become one stepping stone to the 'No Future' critique to come.[37] Post-punk and anarcho-punk were suffused by nuclear disaster syndrome, with almost every crusty band having at least one song about four-minute warnings. (When he discovers the plans for assembling the lead shelter, Rodney, channeling troubled youth in the early series of *Only Fools and Horses*, unloads his anguish on the coming nuclear torture wearing a UK Decay T-shirt). Disaster syndrome was a mass trauma to the eclipsed populations, but a utility for nuclear regimes, since it kept the population formally involved but physically immobile. Nuclear madness also reserved a particular punishment for those clinging to physical defence but who were no longer needed in a post-industrial world. In J.B. Priestley's TV play *Doomsday for Dyson* (1957), a father obsesses over the events leading to the current crisis while looking for the courage to kill his family when the blast comes.[38] The image is gratefully absorbed by Martin Amis in 1987 in his story collection *Einstein's Monsters* (1987), whose contemplation of child-killing among the rubble is used as an epigraph by Julie McDowall in her 2024 account of Cold

---

37   James Thompson, *Psychological Aspects of Nuclear War* (Chichester: British Psychological Society and John Wiley and Sons, 1985 (1983)), vi–vii, 11, 18–19, 31, 39; Steven Kull, *Minds at War: Nuclear Reality and the Inner Conflict of Defence Policymakers* (New York: Basic, 1988). Also British Medical Association, *The Medical Effects of Nuclear War* (Chichester: John Wiley and Sons, 1983).
38   Wr. J. B. Priestley, dir. Silvio Narizzano, *Doomsday for Dyson* (Granada, 1958).

War preparation, *Attack Warning Red*![39] In Kurosawa Akira's film *Ikimono no kiroku/I Live in Fear* (1955), a foundry owner tries to relocate his family to Brazil, the only place he believes to still be safe, and ends up on a psychiatric ward.[40] And in Tim O'Brien's novel *The Nuclear Age* (1985), a father deranged with worry digs a pointless hole in his garden as his family watch.[41] The many iterations of this lesson all stress what Scarry describes as the loss of physical involvement, the need to give up to feedback those loved ones who can't be saved, least of all by those whose labour has been lost to the rational streamlining of *Stepping Stones*.

Perhaps the most telling story of nuclear madness of all is Tom McGrath's entry in the *Play for Today* spinoff series *Play for Tomorrow*, *The Nuclear Family* (1982). In McGrath's story, a former labourer in a post-work future (Jimmy Logan, celebrity Scottish comic actor perhaps best known from *Carry On Abroad*) vainly tries to teach his children about the dignity of labour by taking them on a work-themed holiday to Faslane nuclear base. At Faslane, though, there are harsh lessons for the would-be patriarch, as a naval officer explains that nuclear madness is the real source of both his angst and his back pain:

> It settles inside you and wraps its tentacles around your bones... We stand on a narrow ledge on the highest slope of time. We feel dizzy. A fatal sense of self-destruction pulls us down to disaster, vertical. The fear of the holocaust possesses us.[42]

---

39   Martin Amis, *Einstein's Monsters* (London: Jonathan Cape, 1987).

40   Wr. Hashimoto Shinobu, Hayasaka Fumio, and Kurosawa Akira, dir. Kurosawa Akira, *Ikimono no kiroku*, Tōhō, 1955.

41   Tim O'Brien, *The Nuclear Age* (London: Collins, 1985).

42   Wr. Tom McGrath, dir. John Glenister, *The Nuclear Family*

Nuclear madness is at heart the recognition that the fighting-working body is redundant, that it has been removed by a virtuous feedback loop; and here, this realisation is written onto the body of the Glasgow proletarian, once the backbone of industry, now suffering precisely from a broken back, or what Thomas Moynihan calls 'spinal catastrophism'.[43] Perpetual emergency works its way through the nervous system of the vertebrate, hardwiring fight-or-flight and narrowing the attention — all good for market realism. As James Thompson points out, people become useless in nuclear panic, since their bodies are so hormonally flooded — and in fact this helplessness allows for them to be more effectively treated as objects for nuclear barter. Attention is shredded by panic — the capitalist shrinking of concentration leading to the 'cancellation of the future' described by Fisher and by Raymond Williams before him — and as Thompson and other psychologists described, this acculturates a deep sense of helplessness before unanswerable threats. Open-ended total threat means absolute vulnerability to the blast and to the automating feedback loop.[44] This should be added to the 'No Future' critique of the economy: nuclear madness looks much like helplessness before neoliberal automation. (*Threads*: 'In these early stages, the symptoms of radiation sickness and the symptoms of panic are identical').

The nuclear psy-op leads to nuclear madness being accepted and even demanded as security. In the great end-civilisation securitisation, population uselessness becomes self-fulfilling, a learned helplessness that distracts from

---

(BBC, 1982).

43   Thomas Moynihan, *Spinal Catastrophism: A Secret History* (Falmouth: Urbanomic, 2019).

44   Beck and Bishop, 'Introduction' to Beck and Bishop, *Cold War Legacies*, 25.

wider survival mechanisms such as working towards nuclear disarmament. 'What is that thing just beyond the edges of the mind?' McGrath's frustrated patriarch wonders, what is it that exerts so much control over the nervous system, yet can't be fought. The paralysis, Baden Offord says, comes from

> living with the possibility of nuclear war... paralysing our mind-set to respond adequately. We have chosen to ignore the facts at the heart of the nuclear program with its dangerous algorithm... the techno-industrial-national powers that claim there is 'no immediate danger' ad infinitum.[45]

This is the familiar, everyday, free-floating anxiety whose energy could be repurposed except that the permanent explosion has such power over the attention. Feedback strips out signals that might lean towards repurposing, and channels existing information back in. Feedback streamlines value-mining, stripping out analogue signals and biological interference, and makes the embrace of exterminism a strange patriotic virtue. The everyday misery of feedback-as-communication is the result of this, as surely as the difficulty of voicing political desire for nuclear disarmament. Behind the everyday misery of feedback lies the reminder of the expendability of populations already assumed by the nuclear weapons regime.

---

45   Baden Offord, 'Beyond Our Nuclear Entanglement: Love, Nuclear Pain and the Whole Damn Thing', *Angelaki* 22–3, 2017, 17–25: 18.

TRANSPARENT NUKES

There is a big problem in post-Cold War nuclear cultures' tendency towards retro. The end of the Cold War did not eliminate nukes' job of commanding space, and nuclear stockpiles still hadn't been reduced much even a decade or so after the 'end of history'. Stockpiles declined, then diversified to correspond to American policy, then rose again, by which time they had largely sunk from popular view, with the culture wars sliding in to take their place. Nukes' sinking into the unconscious was really enabled by the free rein given to the empire of evaluation, now able, via information management, to extend its unified light to individuals before the mediating screen. The nuclear threat never disappeared, but was just — as Milne and Kinsella put it — 'allowed to disseminate and radiate beneath the radar of public scrutiny and protest'.[1] The period after the Cold War, and the virtual free rein of American defence and infotech, became an apotheosis of the destruction of physical stakes, collapsing political attention into individual value, most familiarly in the imperative of identity.

Millennial identity politics is an expected outcome of the enhanced imperative of evaluation, demanding a uniformity of space, a Newtonian 'absolute space' in which all points are equivalent and interchangeable.[2] Looking

---

1   Kinsella and Milne, 'Nuclear Theory Degree Zero', in eds. Kinsella and Milne, *Nuclear Theory Degree Zero*, 1–16, 3.

2   In this, Kyoto agreed with, and partly presaged, the Heidegger

back over the millennium, the mutual dependency of a concentration on identity and terminal American hegemony seems obvious; as liberalism becomes performative, empathy becomes currency, the empathetic self assumes a moral high ground, and a post-industrial economy produces typologies that reproduce the tendency of nukes to abstract violence as market abritration. In the first couple of decades of the twentieth century, American power relied on a barrage of moral identity claims working through a soft power that spread from Disney franchises to highbrow university presses. Soft power expanded to cover aerospace concerns, combining extinction-range violence, individual affirmation, and the production of digital identities made compulsory. Nukes anchored the abstraction of violence, but themselves became transparent, perfectly incorporated into the empire of unified space, impossible to pick out from the regime itself. The recommendations of digital detox that pepper post-2010s lifestyle columns, nevertheless, rarely consider the role of the sublimating weapons sitting in the mind as an extinction unconscious and quietly eviscerating other futures.

Commentators on nuclear culture have described how, from the mid-1990s, the imagination of nuclear war would become increasingly detached from real, ongoing nuclear dangers. Nukes' effects were largely sealed off in a discrete past, in a wave of cultural production beginning, not coincidentally, around the point Fisher and others have associated with the rise of retro and the suffocation of newness. Jonathan Hogg describes a shrinking of nuclear culture to nuclear kitsch as 'the nuclear present is rendered invisible'.[3] This involved nuclear danger taking on comfortingly distanced, ironic, or cute forms: the mushroom clouds in

---

of 'The Era of the World Picture' (1938).

3   Jonathan Hogg, *British Nuclear Culture: Official and Unofficial*

the neo-'50s nuclear-family cartoon *The Simpsons* (1989–), or the imagery of the *Fallout* game series (1997–).[4] The reworking of Cold War anxieties as retro acted a great catharsis, and allowed the period from the late nineties to the late noughties to be portrayed, in the Anglosphere at least, as a relatively uneventful decade, even as a great growth in 'global' measurement-and-command extended Cold War technic into an American infotech regime.

At the heart of this cultural deactivation are the hollowed-out remakes that would lead to the 'franchise' version of Hollywood storytelling. The 1959 film *On the Beach*, based on Nevil Shute's 1957 novel about Australians waiting for death by radiation after a war in the Northern hemisphere, took on, in a 2000 remake, a soft-focus for-TV tone and a strange timelessness. This is the timelessness Fisher describes of Adele, the original worked over for maximal value until a complete unmooring from the grain of any historical experience. When the great drama of automated protocols, *Fail Safe*, was revisited in 2000, it was set in a version of the '60s — not a set of stylistic nods to the '60s, but a scene-by-scene repetition of the original story and dialogue, in black and white. Even a cast including Walter Cronkite, Richard Dreyfuss, and George Clooney couldn't stop the 'new' *Fail Safe* from standing as a weird period piece belonging to no period, a pale marker of the end of history. American soft power makes this a persistent paradigm; '60s nuclear remakes would hang on into the 'third nuclear era', as in the adaptation of *Doctor Strangelove* as a film of the stage play with Steve Coogan playing Peter Sellars, whose publicity states, with marked vagueness, that 'it's still important'. This statement has a strangely hollow

---

Narratives in the Long Twentieth Century (London: Bloomsbury, 2016), 169.

4   Hogg, *British Nuclear Culture*, 172, 164–9.

feel in a period when nuclear danger is greater than at any time in the twentieth century. It's a habitual, performative statement, one that leaks the difficulty of noticing concrete dangers.

This is not to say that there are no attempts to imaginatively render immediate dangers in the third nuclear era. Annie Jacobsen's rigorously researched *Nuclear War: A Scenario*, for example, gathers evidence from professionals in the exterminism industries — intelligence officers, Pentagon insiders, nuclear planners, and technicians — to paint a picture of the way in. Elliott Ackerman and James Stavridis's novel *2034* (2021) carefully outlines routes to war from a military viewpoint, repeatedly stressing American overreach and decline.[5] The wider cultural background, though, is one in which a seamless repackaging of the past works against any interruption of the absolute continuity demanded by nuclear realism. Nuclear realism is the silent backing to the Marvel Cinematic Universe, with its performative conflicts fought out on identity grounds, and its promise of perpetual self-actualisation. A continuously recycled culture loses historical anchoring; it is without action or moral purpose, is market driven and historiographically static. It demands perpetual deathless continuity, a continuity picked up by the actual deathliness of Nuclear Gothic (or the actual deathliness of Japan's slide from obedient member of Anglosphere commercial empire as marked by the wave of suicides following the death of Emperor Meiji. The body that is, in Grafton Tanner's term, 'foreverised', is the body anchored by the nuke, removed from history, placidly waiting for the accident it disavows.[6]

Unsurprisingly, the dramatic power of classic nuclear

5   Elliott Ackerman and James Stavridis, *2034: A Novel of the Next War* (London: Penguin, 2024 (2021))

6   Grafton Tanner, *Foreverism* (Cambridge: Polity, 2023).

films is difficult to regain after nukes have been rendered transparent. Millennial Hollywood looked straight through real nukes to create the costume nukes of the Cold War dramas. Yet alongside the adaptation of the post-9/11 American nuclear arsenal for multiple strategic scenarios with multiple possible yields, Hollywood soft power was taking on more seriously global proportions, with most of its rapid economic growth accounted for by international expansion. Globalised, identity-driven Hollywood was the unified light the ultimate weapon dreamed of; and its ultimate means was the franchise film (Harry Potter, Lord of the Rings, Pirates of the Caribbean, the Marvel Universe). The franchise was familiarity, endlessly smoothed and shorn of antagonisms, the acculturation of a self-updating progressive mode, or repetition with minimal variation, as Fisher had it.

The identity-extinction complex would by this point need constant, hybrid, war, a war in which nuclear weapons are constantly being used as part of a spectrum of measures. It needs what H. Bruce Franklin has described as a shift from the 'good war' to the 'forever war', with Soviet communism replaced by liquid enemies, abstractions like the 'War on Terror'.[7] For Hollywood, the nuclear aggressor would now be the isolated terrorist threatening the American world-system. In Phil Alden Robinson's thriller *The Sum of All Fears* (2002) — based on Tom Clancy's 1991 novel about a Palestinian loose nuke — an Austrian billionaire with a homemade device tries to provoke an all-out US-Russian war, and can only be stopped by the franchise hero Jack Ryan. In Gregor Jordan's torture-porn film *Unthinkable* (2010), an Islamic convert, played by an oddly cast but intense Michael Sheen, threatens to detonate hidden

---

7   H. Bruce Franklin, *Crash Course: From the Good War to the Forever War* (New Brunswick, NJ: Rutgers University Press, 2018).

nukes, leaving the American secret service to unleash their righteous anger. In these stories of rogue actor versus secret service hero, the empire's own reliance on nuclear threat, and its openness to eventual accident, is effectively lost, and the only dangerous nukes are loose nukes.

The millennial 'forevering' of the nuclear arsenal, the great abstract war, was explicitly reacting, of course, to the September '01 attack on the spiritual centre of the American empire. Manhattan was not only a world centre of American financial power and a degree zero for millennial aspirational propaganda, it had also long been an anchor of the nuclear regime. Manhattan had given its name to the project to complete the first bomb, named after the influence of Columbia-based scientists — and had often been imagined in superweapon stories as a target in a tradition running through sources as various as Upton Sinclair's *The Millennium* (1924), Judith Merril's *Shadow on the Hearth* (1950), Eugene Burdick and Harvey Wheeler's *Fail Safe* (1962), Whitley Strieber and James Kunetka's *Warday* (1984), and Xavier Gens's *The Divide* (2011).[8] After various Democrat leaders proved themselves effectively unwilling to denuclearise, in the 2010s Donald Trump appealed to the American public as a 'New York guy' rather than a 'Washington guy', casting government as business and insisting that the world order was still a kind of Manhattan project.

This world centre of finance and soft power was even imagined as nuclear target in Alfonso Cuarón's 2006 adaptation of P.D. James's *Children of Men* — a post-nuclear drama rarely remembered as one, presenting a chaotic

---

8   Franklin, *Crash Course*, 14; Tim Street, *The Politics of Nuclear Disarmament: Obstacles to and Opportunities for Eliminating Nuclear Weapons* (Abingdon: Routledge, 2021), 153, 159; Ritchie, *Trident and British Identity*, 6.

struggle with Anglosphere state power in an alternate version of the security/terrorism story.[9] The extreminist story of *Children of Men* describes the empty present of neoliberal London stretched into a security nihilism that captures the No Future condition — no future, no progressive time, no children, no reason for activism. A future London is without future shock — more dirt, more permacrisis, more discordant advertising, more apocalyptic individualism suffused by the extinction unconscious. In some sense, the film is darkly reworking the transatlantic romance so prominent around the millennium — an Anglo-American couple reunite; they remember their activist past and their dead child; and she mentions that her parents were killed in the nuclear centre of the Anglosphere, but registers this as just 'the world we live in'. The 'nuclear Atlantic romance' had been presaged in the recent iteration of the Thatcher-Reagan special relationship, renewed in the post-9/11 British willingness to believe in the 2003 'dodgy dossier' put together by a Labour communications team and claiming an imminent threat, enabling a new London-New York nuclear securitisation.

The adaptation of the American nuclear arsenal after 2001–02 for a wider range of scenarios meant a 're-globalisation' of threat, dissipated and multicentred and often subconscious, and more resilient and permanent than the Mutually Assured Destruction of the Cold War. Extinction-range launch was still possible — the *Threads* scenario was slightly distanced but had never gone away — but threats were complex, constant, and hard to parse. 2001–02 had also seen a shift towards lower-yield war-

---

9   Wr. Alfonso Cuaron, Timothy J. Sexton, David Arata, *Children of Men*, Universal, 2006.

heads, multiple threads of nuclear strategy and hybrid war in which the use of nuclear weapons was technically easier but more difficult to conceptualise.[10] At one end of this spectrum, nuclear bombing existed in a continuum with the 'shock and awe' bombing seen in Iraq and in the 1945 Japanese bombings.[11] The 2002 American Nuclear Posture Review identified seven countries against which the use of nuclear weapons could be justified, including powers with no serious nuclear programmes themselves (Iraq, Libya, Syria — soon followed by George W. Bush's 'axis of evil' speech).[12] The 2002 National Security Strategy included the interventionist demand that other powers could be made to accept 'the benefits of policies that generate higher productivity and sustained economic growth', linking nuclear force to economic pressure.[13] In an era of sensory overload co-ordinated by the infotech/culture-industry beneficiaries of the Cold War, the nuclear imagination was largely submerged. Joseph Masco describes the post-9/11 era as echoing the post-Hiroshima era in terms of a cognitive challenge:

> Both projects involved the designation of new insecurities, new institutions to fight them, a public mobilisation campaign grounded in fear, and above all, official claims that a new kind of war... was a multi-generational commitment, constituting a new mode of everyday life rather than a brief intensity of conflict.[14]

---

10   Walker, *A Perpetual Menace*, 108.

11   Walker, *A Perpetual Menace*, 81, 124.

12   Walker, *A Perpetual Menace*, 169.

13   The White House, The National Security Strategy, 2002: georgewbush-whitehouse.archives.gov/nsc/nss/2002/nss6.html

14   Joseph Masco, *The Theater of Operations: National Security Affect from the Cold War to the War on Terror* (Durham NC:

The Cold War meanwhile, as Beck and Bishop put it, would continue in 'the collapse of the distinction between civilian and soldier; the dependence of the economy on military spending; the foreclosure of the future by nuclear dread; the military origins of the internet'.[15] The nuclear imagination is exhausted in the face of a combined information war, multi-sited and low-barrier proxy wars, and nukes that are strangely bereft of anti-nuclear action.

'Big apocalypse', then, never goes away, but it gets buried in noise and mixed with other more complicated threats. Struggling to tease apart the inputs, the post-2001 Atlantic nuclear imagination sometimes took refuge in the individual-driven story, which made nuclear war a narrative proposition to ground character arcs: the CBS show *Jericho* (2006–08), for example, based in two feuding towns, Jericho and New Bern, the former infiltrated and turned into an oligarchical police state while smalltown America struggles to pull itself together.[16] *Jericho* is full of neat stylisation and mappings of domestic anxieties, yet its post-apocalypse Kansas undergoes inconveniences on the scale of rolling power cuts or lockdowns, while characters keep evolving, estranged even from the narrative challenges of the relatively anodyne *The Day After*, the earlier Kansas story that had galvanised President Reagan. Character-driven realism always struggles with consideration of nuclear horror, and even a film as accomplished as *Oppenheimer* (2023) has to be made as a biopic, since if it wasn't about one

---

Duke University Press, 2014), 5 — quoted in Beck and Bishop, 'Introduction' to *Cold War Legacies*, 16.

15   Beck and Bishop, 'Introduction' to Beck and Bishop *Cold War Legacies*, 24.

16   Cr. Stephen Chbosky, Josh Schaer, Jonathan E. Steinberg, various writers and directors, *Jericho* (CBS, 2006–08).

individual American, it wouldn't trigger any emotions. *Hunger Games*–type young-adult semi-apocalypses also proliferate. *How I Live Now* (2013), based on a 2004 story, sees a precocious New Yorker visit England and find love and knitwear, only to happen on a nuclear attack, taken as a test of character; a nuclear theme laid onto the NATO romcom of *Notting Hill*. This story realises trauma and disorientation — the eerie wind signalling the blast to puzzled children, for example — but is anchored in a coming-of-age relationship. If the narrative framework for the popular nuclear war drama during the late Cold War had been docudrama, in these stories it is the thriller romance.

What the realist thriller-romance story struggles to see is nukes' tendency to depersonalise and denarrativise. The instant war reduces all to simultaneity. Nuclear war really has no time for character arcs, since its world is a world without story, a world in which all *teloi* are buried in non-sequential data, a low-attention world driven by the imperative of value. Nuclear hegemony carries American Cold War imperatives through to post–Cold War monopolies in infotech and mass culture, and a general assault on the attention. Constant nuclear crisis attacks any political ambitions that need a long view and a sustained cultural memory. The lack of attention nailed down by the attention economy and the ceding of culture to retro instills a fear of the loss of continuity, or a fear of a re-entry into history, with all its risks of loss and death, and this is how nuclear security needs it to be. The deathless world is the world of Lockean liberalism, for which experienced time has to be repackaged as the time of production and financial expectation. Inevitably, this tends to a foreverised culture, and in a foreverised culture it is difficult to build the collectivity and consideration needed to even bring up nuclear disarmament. It is not that nuclear disarmament is being decided against, but that it doesn't come up. The idea of a world without nuclear threat is effectively shadow-banned.

Nuclear war, then, favours the stream of data rather than the narrative. And the nuclear threat allows the de-narrativised world to stay in place. The length of a nuclear war, from detection and reaction, is vanishingly small. It is really a race to simultaneity, binding up in its threat the eraseure of time to think. There's no nuclear *War and Peace*, no nuclear *Casablanca*, and, for that matter, no nuclear *London Can Take It!*, there is just a brief unfolding around a single unreal moment, then the reflection on that moment stretching across the cold dark millennia. Cold War stories tended to understand this; in the global-American post–Cold War world, the temporal challenge becomes harder to articulate. The overwhelming simultaneity of nuclear threat, its desire to empty out time, is a major narrative challenge. Cold War stories sometimes answered this by looking back from a future-primitive time onto a blast that has taken on mythological status — *Riddley Walker*; William L. Miller's *A Canticle for Leibowitz* (1959); or, in an important Russian example of post-Cold War thinkability, the Moscow of Tatyana Tolstaya's *The Slynx* (2000)). *The War Game* and *Threads* both show disorientingly shuffled temporalities, with the nuclear eternal always making the present seem unreal. *Threads* builds up the stuff of social realism in a 'kitchen-sink' story of class negotiations — between the family of the working-class boy and the family of his pregnant middle-class girlfriend — only to let these narratives crash and leave behind detritus, individual meaning as fraying narrative threads. But since the romance thriller keeps trying to reconstruct narrative, it relies on intentions that have no real place in the constant emergency, and can't register the violence done to memory by the nuclear threat.

The kind of young-adult noodling seen in *How I Live Now* also risked delaying trauma for some later time, when the play of character types would give way to an admission that nuclear threat had been pushed too far into the unconscious. One nice play on this is in the 2022 conversation between the historian Ashley Jackson and Diane Morgan's character Philomena Cunk. Here, the professor causes Cunk to realise that nuclear weapons haven't disappeared, making her visibly upset and causing her to change the subject to the hits of ABBA.[17] There's more to this than laughing at thick millennials — there's the realisation that we've all been complicit in the forgetting, addicted to distraction and retro while the nuclear Pax Americana consolidated its power. (And it's worth noticing that Diane Morgan herself has a range of lesser-known 2000s hipster characters with Alistair Green who mistake their own identity-performance for radicalism).[18]

Overcoming the transparency of nukes is still the challenge. Even well into the third nuclear age — especially with pressure from publishers and broadcasters to provide content with widespread appeal, and often with a 'flat' global aesthetic — serious writing still sometimes struggles to pull free from the retro of *Fallout*. Julie McDowall's 2024 book *Attack Warning Red* is a crucial digest of domestic British preparations during the Cold War threat laudably arranged for readerly engagement, but is saddled with an overarching tone of retro-quaint. And the book's long subtitle, *How Britain Prepared for Nuclear War*, makes us wonder when Britain *stopped* preparing. (The short title is a retro dog whistle as well, if knowingly so, the phrase '*Attack Warning Red*' being familiar from the incoming strike in *Threads*). The 2024–25 French exhibition *L'Age Atomique* was an

---

17   BBC, *Cunk on Earth*, ep.4, 20 Sept 2022.

18   Among others, Lizard and Latrine: youtube.com/watch?v=q6t-phJd4vf4

outstanding collection of nuclear imageries going right back to early twentieth-century millenarianism, radiation research and modernist art, but it still hits a hiatus post-Cold War and leaves us wondering when '*l'âge*' was. While the exhibition was running, a number of European governments were producing pamphlets preparing populations for conflict with Russia.[19] The nomenclature of a 'third nuclear age' was itself proliferated by a 2024 admission by the British chief of defence, and European countries were trying to get their populations used to the virtues of nuclear rearming — France's hypersonic missiles for example, or the nervous ambitions of Poland.[20]

Less-substantial features and documentaries sometimes seem, Cunk-like, to be seeing transparent nukes for the first time. One marker of this frozen imagination is the citing of warhead yields in multiples of the Hiroshima blast, even though megaton yields have been normal for 70-odd years. Another is a frisson of '80s strangeness acting as a kind of catharsis — *Threads* horror; suburban families building their own shelters in *Protect and Survive* magazine; the various oddities collected in McDowall's *Attack Warning Red*;

---

19   Le Figaro, 'Un manuel de survie en cas de crise majeure va être distribué aux Français', 18 March 2025: lefigaro.fr/actualite-france/un-manuel-de-survie-en-cas-de-crise-majeure-va-etre-distribue-aux-francais-20250318; Swedish Civil Contingencies Agency, 'In Case of Crisis or War': rib.msb.se/filer/pdf/30874.pdf. 'Keep this brochure in a safe place', says the Swedish one, oddly echoing the Cold War guides.

20   Danica Kirka, 'Senior UK military commander warns of a "third nuclear age"', 6 December 2024: https://apnews.com/article/admiral-radakin-defense-nukes-76f37aa34ceafff-d6a9895d23547320b; Associated Press, 'President Duda calls on US to place nuclear weapons in Poland', 13 March 2025: apnews.com/article/poland-duda-nuclear-52c2d921645154539a7778b11d92554b

or the 2019 *Arena* documentary *A British Guide to the End of the World*. Mushroom cloud imagery, once a marker of constant maddening terror, came to work something like an emoji. Library pictures of explosions are rolled out by the *Daily Mail* and the *Mirror* to be placed next to 'Trump/ Putin threatens...', with the expectation of desensitisation and a quick moving on of the shredded attention. The problem here isn't imagery from the past — images from the past are crucial — it's that the images are made retro by lifting them out of any historical embedding for a contracting new cycle. A dissociated mushroom cloud doesn't tell us anything about nuclear threats, how nukes carve out domestic and international empires, or whether we can say anything to them; it makes the issue unreal. The import of the mushroom cloud has long since been lost. Mushroom clouds are d'oh.

If the challenge of nuclear transparency was taken up anywhere widely and seriously in the 2010s, it was less in the pop culture where it should have thrived than in the space of the art exhibition. The works collected by the Nuclear Culture Research Project, for example, often address the invisible penetration of radionuclides into biological life, as well as the gap between narrowing attention capabilities and unimaginably long nuclear timescales.[21] The Atomic Priesthood Project, for example, draws from an older mini-field of speculative linguistics that considers how to convey danger over vast periods ('nuclear semiotics'): people's relationship with duration is irrevocably warped by the nuclear threat, while nuclear awareness requires a mythopoesis of radionuclides 'on geologic timescales through the use of ritual, allegory, and superstition'.[22] In 1968 Stanislaw Lem,

---

21   Nuclear Culture group: nuclear.artscatalyst.org

22   The Atomic Priesthood Project: theatomicpriesthoodproject. org

author of *Solaris*, imagined satellites carrying warning messages about radiation for future humans; Matthew Kielty's 'Ray Cats' project — reviving Françoise Bastide and Paolo Fabbri's idea of a living radioactivity detector — imagines far-future cats genetically modified to change colour to warn humans of danger, a provocation about communicability and time that would spread into merch ('The movement and process is bigger than the cats').[23] Robert Williams and Bryan McGovern Wilson's *Cumbrian Alchemy* (2012–14) is a nuclear psychogeography aimed at a memory of radioactive waste on the landscape of northwest England.[24] The dyeing or making-perceptible of radionuclides from waste or accidents is another thread of 2010s gallery work: sculptures made from leaked radioactive material or plants carrying isotopes. At the same time, some of the 'spent material' work, particularly galvanised by the Fukushima accident of 2011, risks overlooking the political import of the nuclear cycle, in the ways energy and weapons get connected. Nuclear power can be acted on and improved; but the use of radionucludes for weapons is a deeply ingrained habit that needs to be made visible as a political process, with implications much greater than the persistence of any given isotope.

'Nuclear anthropocene art', though, keeps open the question of invisibility, where weapons production largely disappears in the wider culture. For latter-day 'nuclearism', or language that naturalises nukes, the threat of totalised violence is inevitable at a certain point in human develop-

---

23   Stanislaw Lem, trans. Seth Shostak, *Głos Pana/His Master's Voice* (Cambridge MA: MIT Press, 2020 (1968)); The Ray Cats Solution: theraycatsolution.com/#10000

24   *Cumbrian Alchemy*: nuclear.artscatalyst.org/content/cumbrian-alchemy. Cumbria had been extensively surveyed for disposal since the 1980s.

ment; it has to be relegated to the unconscious as a condition of modernity, and it is held to demonstrate, as Pelopidas says, 'a layer of irreversibility in human history'.[25] As early as Wells's *The World Set Free*, the atomic weapon had been seen as a cascading of present violence into eternity, a temporal shift imaged by the open-endedness of the chain reaction, or what Wells calls the 'continuing explosive', 'a blazing continual explosion'.[26] This irreversibility marks the 'No Alternative' hardening of a singular, universal time of progress. It marks the temporary crisis that is effectively permanent. Similarly, Pelopidas describes how, although 2000s governments never officially let go of a nuclear-weapons-free world, they came to see this as a 'dream' that could be relegated to 'a future that is officially desirable but in practice can never come'.[27] Culturally, this perpetual diversion from the future depends on algorithmic siloing and the stretching of a perpetual empty present over the kind of memory described by *Cumbrian Alchemy*.

Pelopidas powerfully reads this detached, nuclear-free future in President Obama's Prague speech of 2009. Despite calls to push towards nuclear zero from figures as unlikely as Henry Kissinger and George Schultz, the Obama administration saw disarmament as belonging to a future that 'will not be reached quickly — perhaps not in my lifetime'.[28] As Pelopidas says, disarmament is here reduced to a rhetorical question, to 'hopeful pronouncements with

---

25   Pelopidas, 'The Birth of Nuclear Eternity', 484.

26   Wells, *The World Set Free*, 39.

27   Pelopidas, 'The Birth of Nuclear Eternity', 484.

28   George P. Schultz, William J. Perry, Henry A. Kissinger, and Sam Nunn, 'A World Free of Nuclear Weapons', *Wall Street Journal*, 4 Jan 2007: https://www.wsj.com/articles/SB116787515251566636; Benoît Pelopidas, 'The Birth of Nuclear Eternity', 488; William Walker, 'The UK, threshold status and

no concern for their plausible implementation', effectively making it impossible to disarm.[29] Hillary Clinton's wording during the 2010 negotiation of the New Strategic Arms Reduction Treaty (New START) is even starker. Here the secretary of state describes her own dream of 'some century, free of nuclear weapons' — meaning that even in the best circumstances, the world's most powerful military (controlled by increasingly unpredictable governments) is absolutely locked into developing extinction weapons for centuries to come.[30] A commitment to the progressive march towards the certain accident can never be official, the moment of disarmament is postponed 'beyond [any] horizon, which is enough to reproduce nuclear eternity whether or not one imagines it'.[31]

As Pelopidas describes elsewhere, the acceptance of this condition as neutral and transparent depends on the decline of cultural forms that can make their violence thinkable.[32] Without a serious struggle to depict their actual violence, they become inevitable by default. Nor can this condition be reached by what Peter Watkins called the cultural 'monoform'. Watkins's own answer points forwards to the '80s cultural wave I've called Nuclear Gothic — culture that tries to break through the perfect abstraction of violence in nuclear weapons, to show the real physical violence they promised. Nuclear Gothic often reworked the conventions of realism — *Threads*' *Taste of Honey*–like awkward cross-class pregnancy, for example — but it was

responsible nuclear sovereignty', *International Affairs* 86–2, 2010, 447–64.

29   Pelopidas, 'The Birth of Nuclear Eternity', 488.

30   Pelopidas, 'The Birth of Nuclear Eternity', 488.

31   Pelopidas, 'The Birth of Nuclear Eternity', 490.

32   Pelopidas, 'Imaginer la possibilité de la guerre nucléaire pour y faire face'.

also often genuinely Gothic, depicting violent or deathly forces that had supposedly been civilised away, and echoing the 1790s rise of the Gothic novel alongside the British reassertion of absolute continuity against the French Revolution and the claim that Britain was aloof from European violence. Against Pelopidas's nuclear eternal, the Gothic marks embodiment, death, violence, sex (*Threads* begins with Ruth's implied impregnation on a Sheffield hillside — the pregnancy will echo down for two generations of birth defects before reaching the end of its own narrative). Gothic is a return to the body amid abstractions. The absolute continuity in British natural law promises that all physical conflict will be sublimated in a deactivated future; Nuclear Gothic introduces a present-tense visceral jolt that disturbs this depoliticisation. The hauntology of *Cumbrian Alchemy* inherits this Gothic sensibility — though the making-opaque of nuclear pollution tackled by this kind of art too rarelye extends into the realm of the nuclear weapons unconscious. The space-unifying weapon, for its possessors, has to be constantly distanced from the ground of the political to become invisible — and it has to eviscerates the ground of the political entirely. Even when real disarmament questions are raised, they often fail to be seen as such. This is exactly what happened in public debates over self-determination in the 2010s.

NUKES VERSUS
SELF-DETERMINATION

Those of us interested in nuclear cultural history have often arrived there through some kind of trauma prompted by dramas of the present horror, typically *Threads*. The children forced into a state of helplessness by the revelation of the horrors coming at any point should be listened to — they are Cold War veterans, people with real injuries planned for them from above. This wasn't what happened in my case: it was only after seeing them much later that the force of dramas like *Threads* and *The War Game* became obvious. There might have been something about growing up pointed towards Prestwick Airport, a major nuclear target. But the real catalyst was an interest in Scottish independence, and realising the gap in attitudes towards nukes across the border, with disarmament questions seeming normal to the north, while rarely coming up in rUK (the rest of the UK). Almost anyone who's been through Scottish independence campaigns will see nuclear weapons as a great unspoken element in British politics, and will see the naturalness of nukes as depending on an unusual constitutional form. Nukes are regularly sold to the public as a defence of national sovereignty, but what they really do is fix the ultimate form of that sovereignty where it can be protected from the population. If the machinery of UK parliamentary representation is now broadly mistrusted, if its constitutional inertia is widely understood, scepticism about the form of violence that protects it, in rUK at least, has a way to go.

This rift in the acceptance of nuclear realism can be read across the thermonuclear era, but it accelerated after 1979. Only a couple of months before the election of a Thatcher government, a last-minute amendment had held off the first referendum on devolution, despite 52 percent voting yes. This double defeat would galvanise a sense of belonging specific to a sub-British level, a politicised level. And key among the political threads coalescing in the early '80s would be the alliance between nuclear activism and independence activism. A broad national alliance taking in some of Labour's left would threaten to outflank Labour's British mainstream in nuclear and constitutional scepticism — part of the reason Tony Blair would be so keen to manage devolution desires in the '90s. After 1999, independence thinking and nuclear-sceptical thinking in the Scottish Parliament remained a thorn in the side of British nuclear realism, while rUK criticism would be largely restricted to rogue sectors of the left, Labour rebels, a revived CND, and the Greens. The placement of Britain's nuclear weapons exacerbated the national specificity of this resistance — only 30-odd miles from Scotland's largest city, yet somehow seen as remote. This is the perceived remoteness that would be taken up by Alasdair Gray, the pro-independence icon who describes Glasgow in particular as a lacuna in assurances of representation, and demands a new cultural re-evaluation speaking to a new form of sovereignty.[1] During the 1980s–90s 'cultural renaissance' of which *Lanark*'s plea is sometimes seen as foundational, sovereignty would slide downwards, and nuclear scepticism would come to be more or less assumed.

---

1   Alasdair Gray, *Lanark: A Life in Four Books* (Edinburgh: Canongate, 1979).

If it's true that nuclear deterrence protects government from the population, conversely, population sovereignty pushes against the naturalisation of deterrence. The link between democratic dysfunction and nuclear arsenals has been described by writers including Elaine Scarry, Beatrice Heuser, Tim Street, and Nick Ritchie, who in their various ways all see nuclear empires as depending on the suppression of popular sovereignty. Less often registered by nuclear writers is how popular sovereignty was the explicit crux of Scottish independence: what characterised British authority was not so much rapacious establishment toffs, or an alleged English tendency to vote Tory forever, as the absolute refusal of popular sovereignty. Self-determination campaigns leading to 2014 were carefully channeled by most British media into questions of identity (Are you proud?) or of economy (Can you make it alone?) — which is to say that they underwent the normal reduction to questions of evaluation — but underneath this was the more fundamental question of the sovereignty form standing over the population and wielding absolutely abstracted force.

The absolute sovereignty of parliament is an unusual condition, even if British ideology presents it as universal, or as a great overcoming of kings. Absolute sovereignty makes parliament the sole arbiter of population desires, the cipher of all political representation, or abstraction, funnelling all agency through its arcane mechanisms and its inertia. In classical constitutional commentary, the British constitution — unwritten because it is an expression of nature and arises organically (it is 'discovered, not invented', in Newton's phrase) — should apply evenly across all territories and dominions. The constitution is precisely the dis-placing force carried by the space-unifying weapon. This evenness of British authority across all territories was laid out by the canonical constitutional lawyer A.V. Dicey, who also spent much of his career warning about the abomination of Irish Home Rule.[2] But for a Scottish constitutional counter-tradition posing a critical threat especially after 1979, this Diceyan evenness had never really been established by, or after, the (1700s) Acts of Union. Scottish popular sovereignty remained as a legal force — the population, to borrow Scarry's term for nuclear authority, had not been eclipsed.[3]

If this kind of counter-commentary gathered speed under Thatcherite neoliberalism/nuclearism, it would seem to have reached an unstoppable momentum by the last years of the Cold War. The Constitutional Convention's *Claim of Right* in 1989 described what they saw as a self-evident 'sovereign right of the Scottish people to determine the form of Government best suited to their needs'.[4] This sovereignty was disputed, of course, but the absolute sovereignty of parliament was gradually eroded. Absolute parliamentary sovereignty expects opinion to be fairly easy to channel back towards existing policy; but if, as in Dicey's Celtic nightmare, self-determination seeps in, so do more interruptions. Absolute parliamentary sovereignty, always tending towards constitutional entropy and short-term fixes to affirm existing structures, provided the technocratic substrate in which the H-bomb could flourish; Scottish mixed sovereignty tended to threaten the seal of this inertia, not only for Scotland, but for the nuclear-backed UK itself.

By the mid-2010s, according to some polls, around three quarters of Scottish residents (not independence

---

2   A.V. Dicey, *England's Case Against Home Rule* (London: J. Murray, 1886).

3   Ian McLean, *What's Wrong With the British Constitution* (Oxford: Oxford University Press, 2009), 128–40.

4   Ed. Owen Dudley Edwards, *Claim of Right for Scotland* (Edinburgh: Polygon, 1989).

voters or 'nationalists', but all adults living there) may have considered themselves not in favour of Trident renewal.[5] Disarmament was, and is, the stated policy of the Scottish government. So while it's commonplace in rUK to see nuclear disarmament as loony left opinion or naive on the permacrisis, disarmament thinking has long been common in the country where UK nukes are actually based. Over the millennium, disarmament was closer than many imagined, but it is hard to see through the veil of constitutional naturalism. In 2014, independence, which would almost definitely mean nuclear disarmament, was voted for by 38 percent of Scotland's entire electorate. (For comparison, in 2019 the Conservatives won a general election with the votes of 24 percent of the total electorate, and Labour won a 'landslide' in 2024 with 20 percent).[6] This isn't so much about Scottish oddness, far less 'identity'. It's more about the normalising power of the unwritten British constitution and actual normalness of population nuclear scepticism, *contra* British parliamentary wisdom. The constitutional question unlocks the nuclear question. Disarmament can only be kept unthinkable by all the arcane machineries of absolute parliamentary sovereignty, but at popular sovereignty level it has always been much more serious than a lack of press coverage has suggested. Even two years into the Ukraine War, and despite strong messaging on the effectiveness of nuclear deterrence, a

---

5   Scottish Campaign for Nuclear Disarmament, 'Vote YES and Ban the Bomb', n.d.: banthebomb.org/ne/scotlandnato.pdf; Wallis, *The Truth About Trident*, 157.

6   Scottish Government, The Scottish Independence Bill: A Consultation on an Interim Constitution for Scotland (Edinburgh: Scottish Government, 2014): https://www2.gov.scot/Resource/0045/00452762.pdf; John Ainslie, *Trident: No Place to Go* (London: CND and Scottish CND, 2012).

YouGov survey found that only about half of those polled supported the UK's possession of nuclear weapons.[7]

If nuclear weapons scepticism is the position of even a large minority of the population, it is worth noticing how this large constituency tends to go almost unheard, and is habitually separated from any real political or media efficacy on a UK level. This constituency doesn't fit into any broadcaster guidelines on balance, and it can disappear under first past the post and the party-political system more easily than in other European countries. This large minority is much larger than the 18 percent of MPs — or roughly 9 percent of MPs in UK-committed parties — who opposed Trident in a Commons vote in 2016. This included only 47 of 187 Labour MPs, joined by seven Lib Dems and one Green (Caroline Lucas, like Jeremy Corbyn a CND vice-president), with other votes split according to support for the current form of the British union, and the number of Labour MPs against Trident lower than the number of MPs against the UK state.[8] What this means is that nuclear realism was utterly bound to British parliamentary

---

7   YouGov survey, 'Do you support or oppose the UK having nuclear weapons', 2024: yougov.co.uk/topics/politics/survey-results/daily/2024/01/22/c4fed/1; British Pugwash, '2023 UK public opinion survey on nuclear weapons: article and data': britishpugwash.org/2023-uk-public-opinion-survey-on-nuclear-weapons-article-and-data/.

8   Scottish CND, 'Draft bill shows Yes vote will eject Trident', n.d.: banthebomb.org/index.php/news/trident/1568-draft-bill-shows-yes-vote-will-eject-trident; John Ainslie, *Trident,* 4; Georgia Graham, 'Scottish "yes" vote will force Britain to abandon nuclear weapons', *Telegraph*, 18 March 2014: telegraph.co.uk/news/uknews/scottish-independence/10701826/Scottish-yes-vote-will-force-Britain-to-abandon-nuclear-weapons.html; Timmon Milne Wallis, *The Truth About Trident* (Edinburgh: Luath, 2016), 160.

loyalty. There is no real lack of desire to rethink nuclear arms, but this is held off by institutions clustering around absolute parliamentary sovereignty.

The early history of CND shows that anti-nuclear movements have always tended to operate beyond British parliamentary representation, but the post-1979 era put this onto a level of national agency. Under Neil Kinnock in the mid-'80s, Labour finally learned to love the bomb. The association of unilateralism with unelectability became a core belief, though this association doesn't always stand up, especially since under a first-past-the-post system, with psephology (empirical studies of voting intentions) typically having to assume static lumps of opinion.[9] Soon after Callaghan's acceptance of IMF conditions, followed by Labour's election loss in 1979, Raymond Williams described how, even as Warsaw Pact countries were placing medium-range missiles in Europe, 'in left politics... "the bomb" has for the most part been pushed into the margin of more tractable arguments about political strategy and tactics'.[10] This was less true in Williams's Wales; but no major British Unionist party since has entertained nuclear disarmament strategies, and all have rejected the kind of European collaboration on multilateralism wanted by Williams. (The Green Party is an exception, and continues to advocate for the UK to join the 2017 Treaty on the Pro-

9   Labour Party, General Election Manifesto, 1974: labour-party. org.uk/manifestos/1974/oct/1974-oct-labour-manifesto.shtml; Labour Party, The Labour Party Manifesto, 1987, 15; Kristan Stoddart, *Facing Down the Soviet Union: Britain, the USA, NATO and Nuclear Weapons, 1976–1983* (Basingstoke: Palgrave Macmillan, 2014), 12; Heuser, *Nuclear Mentalities?*, 13; Wallis, *The Truth About Trident*, 195.

10   Williams, 'The Politics of Nuclear Disarmament', 65; Milne, 'Poetry After Hiroshima, 92.

hibition of Nuclear Weapons). When the millennial Tony Blair and Gordon Brown governments claimed not only that the UK was multilateralist, but that its multilateralism was *world-leading*, Britain was nevertheless still committed to American nuclear strategy, and 'world-leading' had more of the smell of neoliberal nation-branding than a desire to put a dent in the permacrisis.[11] 1998 Blair's Strategic Defence Review showed a 'univocal commitment to nuclear weapons' that would be in place at least into the second half of the twenty-first century.[12] By the end of the Brown administration, extinction-range weapons were coming to be seen as a public good, an anchor of a troubled economy. One of Chancellor Alistair Darling's first reactions to the 2007–08 financial crisis was to promote Trident renewal as public investment.[13] The returning Labour administration in 2024–25 would come to see massive drone/AI/nuclear rearming as a protection against stagflation,

---

11   Foreign and Commonwealth Office, *Lifting the Nuclear Shadow*, 2009: media.nti.org/pdfs/55_4.pdf; Cabinet Office, *The Road to 2010: Addressing the Nuclear Question in the Twenty First Century* (Crown Copyright, July 2009), 3. In this they echoed Geoffrey Howe, who under Thatcher had also cast multilateralism as a competitive performance, asking that Britain 'make the running' — Michael J. Turner, *Britain's International Role, 1970–1991* (Basingstoke: Palgrave, 2010), 102.

12   Street, *The Politics of Nuclear Disarmament*, 157; Hogg, *British Nuclear Culture*. 159–60, 162, 171; Wallis, *The Truth About Trident*, 43.

13   Allegra Stratton and Ashley Seager, 'Darling invokes Keynes as he eases spending rules to fight recession', *Guardian*, 20 October 2008: theguardian.com/politics/2008/oct/20/economy-recession-treasury-energy-housing; Walker, 'The UK, threshold status and responsible nuclear sovereignty', 447–64: 458–9.

looking for growth in the promise of becoming a 'defence industrial superpower'.[14]

Much as it had been in 1951, Labour's nuclear enthusiasm would be gratefully inherited by 2010s Conservatives. In 2013, PM David Cameron claimed that nuclear deterrence was needed now 'more than ever' — the kind of performative statement that is naturalised by permacrisis but makes little sense after a glance at Cold War history.[15] The maximum number of British warheads would soon be raised to 260, and as Timmon Milne Wallis describes, UK governments 'voted against, blocked or boycotted virtually every other multilateral nuclear disarmament initiative', opposing work by 189 countries on de-escalation at the 2015 Non-Proliferation Review Conference, and brushing off the legal commitments of the Non-Proliferation Treaty as 'an aspiration'.[16] Like the US and Russia (though not China and India), the UK continues to refuse 'No First Use',

---

14   David Lynch, 'Submarine building at Barrow a 'blueprint' for UK growth, Starmer says', *Evening Standard*, 30 March 2025: standard.co.uk/business/business-news/submarine-building-at-barrow-a-blueprint-for-uk-growth-starmer-says-b1217745.html

15   David Cameron, 'We need a nuclear deterrent more than ever', *Telegraph*, 3 April 2013.

16   Wallis, *The Truth About Trident*, 168–72; Ronald McCoy, 'Afterword', in eds. Douglas Holdstock and Frank Barnaby, *The British Nuclear Weapons Programme, 1952–2002* (Abingdon: Routledge, 2003), 137–44: 141; Street, *The Politics of Nuclear Disarmament*, 40. Non-Proliferation Treaties have often been ignored by nuclear weapons states, as nuclear commentators have pointed out; in 1995 the US rejected the 1948 UN Convention on genocide to argue that the use of nuclear weapons was not illegal — Street, *The Politics of Nuclear Disarmament*, 53, 22; International Court of Justice, *Legality of the Threat or Use of Nuclear Weapons*, 1995: icj-cij.org/case/95

meaning that nuclear escalation could be used against a conventional threat. The only real wobble for nuclear realism among British Party leadership would come after 2015 with the election of CND vice-president Jeremy Corbyn as Labour leader — though by the 2019 General Election Corbyn's initiative had been overcome, and the manifesto saw Labour simply stating its commitment to Trident.[17]

But even if the nuclear-sceptical grassroots of the Labour Party had got their way, it's not certain that any disarming pledge would have survived constitutional entropy in power. This is the scenario explored in *A Very British Coup*, a 1982 novel by Corbyn collaborator Chris Mullin. In Mullin's story, networks of intelligence, finance, civil service and journalism quietly collaborate to frustrate the election promise of a working-class prime minister, introduced in his home in the nuclear-free zone of Sheffield (the Park Hill estate, in the 1988 TV version). Prospective PM Harry Perkins makes superpower non-alignment a cornerstone of his manifesto pledges, and when elected asks American forces to leave, only to be told (like Callaghan) that 'if you kick out our bases, you can kiss goodbye to any help from the United States in putting this ramshackle economy of yours back together'.[18] As Perkins points out to mortified colleagues and civil servants, this nuclear front eternalises the 'neutral' Atlantic and is 'based on the assumption that the only threat to our security comes from the Soviet Union'.[19] But the new PM finds himself frustrated by establishment forces falling into synchrony, including the consensus wing of the labour movement, 'Trade Unionists for Multilateral

---

17   Labour Party Manifesto 2019: labour.org.uk/wp-content/uploads/2019/11/Real-Change-Labour-Manifesto-2019.pdf

18   Chris Mullin, *A Very British Co*up (London: Hodder and Stoughton, 1982), 80, 81.

19   Mullin, *A Very British Coup*, 150–1.

Nuclear Disarmament', with their commitment to Pelopidas's disconnected-future time (or Williams's — '"Multilateralism" is in fact a codeword for continued acquiescence in the policy of military alliances and the arms race').[20] Perkins's cabinet are heavily surveilled by DI5 — a version of DS19, Michael Heseltine's real intelligence agency monitoring CND — and the press play their part in renormalising deterrence, much as in the 1950-60s infiltration scares:

> Ministers were presented as unwitting agents of the Soviet Union... *The Times* said that Britain would never be able to hold her head high again and the *Guardian* commented that while a case might be made out for severing military ties with the United States, now was not the time.[21]

This phrasing — 'Now was not the time' — holding in place the disconnected future, uncannily anticipates the *Guardian*'s later real comment on the disarming threat that was Scottish independence, when its immediately pre-referendum editorial of September 2014 pleaded that 'Britain deserves another chance'.[22] British constitutional change and performative multilateralism belong to the same logic: both are subject to a permanent postponement, desirable but always unrealistic at any given moment. The policies of the Scottish government (scrapping university tuition fees; increasing investment in healthcare; constitutional reform) are the kind of policies the *Guardian* has to seem to support, but they're caught in the bind of 'always not yet'.

---

20   Williams, 'The Politics of Nuclear Disarmament', 34.

21   Mullin, *A Very British Coup*, 173, 169–70.

22   Editorial, 'The Guardian view on the Scottish referendum: Britain deserves another chance', *Guardian*, 12 Sept 2014: theguardian.com/commentisfree/2014/sep/12/guardian-view-scottish-independence?CMP=twt_gu

The temporality of British authority itself is 'not yet'. And 'not yet' is what is carried by the nuclear eternity. Britain always deserves another chance, because Britain is defined by always-another-chance, the endless realist postpone- ment of the apocalypse that is popular sovereignty. For the *Guardian*, 'nationalism is not the answer'. British nation- alism, though, the nationalism that hardwires the nuclear eternal, is not really nationalism, but the universal that stands beyond any nations. Since the British constitution is an expression of nature, support for British parliament's command over all life in perpetuity is not only not national- ist, it can even be the position of those apparently appalled by nationalism. The same paper had recently promoted a letter from 200 celebrity British nationalists (BBC stal- warts, businesspeople, national treasures, other *Guardian* journalists, media folk, etc.) asking Scotland not to give in to nationalism, presented as a question of resentful iden- tity. These national treasures' demand not to disturb the constitutional entropy might be unremarkable, except that these familiar voices were also effectively asking for a per- manent commitment to apocalyptic threat.[23] It's not just that these celebs were guiding the population towards the 2020s British dystopia. More than this, in blocking one of the last offramps for extinction-range weapons, they were demanding an embrace of the inevitable acci- dent and the cold dark millennia, and presenting this as the neutral position.

What is being defended by the celebrities' open letter is sheer continuity — not the continuity of something in particular, but absolute empty continuity itself, the exhaustion of any active present. It marks a *general* secu-

---

23   *The Guardian*, 'Celebrities' open letter to Scotland': theguard- ian.com/politics/2014/aug/07/celebrities-open-letter-scotland-inde- pendence-full-text

ritisation, a condition in which the liberal foundations of the social contract can no longer adapt and instead turn nihilistic — as the Kyoto School could have explained.[24] Politicians become managers policing commitment to habits that have sunk into bureaucratic quicksand, habituated to a language of progress that blocks any meaningful sense of a way forward. Something like this exhaustion of the present is described by Jonathan Schell's classic *The Fate of the Earth* (1982): the extinction threat does not belong to some future time, but is buried within all narratives of meaning and belonging, erasing all past and future generations.[25] The enemy of the nuclear security state isn't so much any particular foreign target as *discontinuity itself*. Or as one 2006 Ministry of Defence statement put it, the 'independent British nuclear deterrent is an essential part of our insurance against the uncertainties and risks of the future'.[26]

One example of the British worship of constitutional stasis I've talked about before is *500 Questions*, a 2013 pamphlet against self-determination that opens with a foreword by the chair of Better Together, Alasdair Darling, who in 2008 had promoted Trident as a necessary public investment.[27] *500 Questions* lists over 500 catastrophic risks arising from the disturbance of constitutional entropy, some of them unintentionally comic ('466. What will Scotland's

---

24   Malcolm Chalmers and William Walker, *Uncharted Waters: The UK, Nuclear Weapons and the Scottish Question* (East Linton: Tuckwell, 2001), 40–1.

25   Jonathan Schell, *The Fate of the Earth* (London: Jonathan Cape, 1982).

26   Ministry of Defence, *The Future of the United Kingdom's Nuclear Deterrent* (London: HMSO, 2006), 5.

27   Better Together, '500 Questions' (independently published, 2013) (later removed from internet).

international dialling code be?'), most involving minor administrative restructuring, and including a whole section warning about an independent Scotland being kicked out of the EU, three years before this mostly Remain-voting region was dragged out by the UK. What makes this obscure pamphlet so telling is its admission that amid the horrors of changing dialling codes and committee names, extinction-range weapons controlled by secret groups of careerists in a dysfunctional polity are not considered a risk. Just the opposite — they are security.

As Beck and Bishop describe, the Cold War need to manage the future, spanning nukes, behaviour, and data processing, had always aimed at an an ultimate securitisation, a 'desire to command and control contingency'.[28] This contingency control also describes the 2010s defence of the nuclear state. Indy 2014 ultimately can be seen as a contest over understandings of time — on one hand, an endless and originless continuity; on the other, a time that is active in the sense of having embodied human stakes. The DIY pro-independence cultural platforms that grew during the campaigns (*National Collective, Bella Caledonia*) were well aware of this temporal battle, often contrasting a possible determinable future with the death spiral of millennial retro that was then also being described by an increasingly influential Mark Fisher. The imagery of these DIY platforms tended to borrow heavily from Gray, the novelist associated — mistakenly, but indicatively — with the injunction to 'live as if in the early days of a better nation'. For there to be a genuinely open, non-determined future, the stranglehold of abstracting violence would have to be broken. Self-determination, in this sense, is really a challenge to think beyond the end of the world.

---

28   Beck and Bishop, 'Introduction' to Beck and Bishop *Cold War Legacies*, 6.

Self-determination might well also shatter British sol-id-state deterrence in a much more concrete way, though: without Scotland's Diceyan consent, there might be no nuclear base at all. An independent Scotland would be un-likely to keep providing staff and facilities at Faslane, and even if rUK were designated (like Russia) a 'successor state' to minimise proliferation issues, building a whole new nuclear base outside Scotland might well be prohibitively expensive.[29] Senior Tories — including Michael Heseltine and John Major — warned that Scottish independence might well mean the end of the British nuclear deterrent. But the end of the British nuclear deterrent was by now a cultural staple of self-determination, so that, as William Walker says, 'the nuclear weapons system designed to guar-antee the UK's survival could hasten its demise'.[30] The 2014 threat — as well as any future threat of self-determination — is likely the most serious challenge to thermonuclear monarchy British history has seen. There's an obvious sign of this in the readiness of the British establishment to recognise the threat and coalesce against it, much as they did in Mullin's *A Very British Coup*: Labour plat-form-shared with UKIP, HMG sock organisations fought the DIY cultural platforms, and the BBC (as Mullins him-self critiques in Perkins's travails) found out how little their neutrality stretched.

Any future push for self-determination, in troubling the natural deterrent, will tend to be seen as a similar existential threat. It will tend to be dismissed as a product of scheming politicians, and will likely be equated with the current am-bitions of political parties, and referred to the current state of the SNP. But not only has self-determination never been

---

29   Chalmers and Walker, *Uncharted Waters*, 78–79, 97–98, 103, 120–34; Wallis, *The Truth About Trident*, 171.

30   Quoted in Wallis, *The Truth About Trident*, 160.

limited to one political party, reducing it to party politics is a way of returning it to British parliamentary realism, with its arcane ways of channeling power.[31] Reports of the decline of Scottish independence after the 2010s have been overstated, and surveys show pro-independence opinion to hover around 47–48 percent.[32] But besides this, self-determination is not a single cathartic moment: it is a direction of travel. Nor is it limited to any one part of the UK. Why have versions of English independence not been more explored as a problem for British nuclear realism? Possibly they will be; possibly nuclear scepticism will be recognised as folk opposition and meet Anglo-localism or latter-day hauntologies, or even just the turn away from Westminster managers.[33] Constitutional inertia as omnicidal: this could have been put more strongly in the 2010s, and should still be put more strongly.

---

31   On devolution in 1999, Scotland adopted the European norm of incorporating a degree of proportional representation in voting — like devolved Wales, London, and Northern Ireland, and, likely, any future England, Yorkshire, or Northern counties. In this, parties become much less authoritative for the nation as a whole.

32   Politics.co.uk, Scottish Independence Poll, 11 March 2024: politics.co.uk/reference/scottish-independence-polls/

33   In terms of the outdatedness of nukes, pointed out by a number of commentators, Ele Carpenter has interestingly described 'tacit knowledge', informal knowledge that is not easily transferred, and suggested that forms of knowledge that are not practiced gradually fall away; nuclear knowledge could become a hauntologically buried knowledge to be put in its time — and this is perhaps part of the point of the *Cumbrian Alchemy* project.

NUKES AS PORNOCRACY

If media theorists are right that new forms of communication emerge out of the technology of the latest war's decisive weapon, it is unsurprising that nuclear standoff grew from a massive expansion of data processing in the 1940s. The Manhattan Project's bomb design depended on vast advancements in information processing. The first assignment of the first general-purpose programmable computer, the ENIAC (Electronic Numerical Integrator and Computer), was a feasibility study for a thermonuclear weapon. Familiarly, the demand for nuclear-survivable networks drove the development of early TCP/IP protocols for the Advanced Research Projects Agency Network (ARPANET).[1] The British 'Backbone' communication network, resilient against nuclear attack, depended on the network of relays that had been created by a massive expansion of the BBC necessary to wartime opinion management.[2] Strategy since the Trinity Tests meant a coalescence of processing powers described by Timothy Ström as a 'unity of communication and control', aiming to 'render... the planet's surface as a general equivalent' — the famil-

1   Timothy Erik Ström, 'Capital and Cybernetics', *New Left Review* 135, May-June 2022, 23–41, 28.
2   John W.P. Phillips, 'Notes from the Underground: Microwaves, Backbones, Party Lines and the Post Office Tower', in eds. Beck and Bishop, *Cold War Legacies*, 213–33: 221–3.

iar unification of space taken as a condition of civilization from Newton and Locke onwards.[3]

Correspondingly, victory in the Cold War paved the way for the global expansion of Silicon Valley's untrammeled role in thought-mapping. Google launched its search engine soon after the Cold War in 1998, then grew explosively. Its holding company, Alphabet, would later diversify into biotech and aerospace; meanwhile, Silicon Valley provides hardware and support for warheads and guidance, and weapons companies like Lockheed Martin have significant presences in infotech.[4] It is not just that 'AI might get hold of nukes' — more fundamentally nuclear regimes have always been based in advanced information management.[5] As Beck and Bishop describe, 'the elaborate technologies of the Cold War emerged in coextension with non-material systems of simulations, optimisation, pattern recognition, data mining and algorithms'.[6] By the 1960s, satellite technology was allowing for a blurring of the boundaries between entertainment, industry and military, in a coalescence of space-managing technologies.[7] As Beck and Bishop put it,

---

3   Ström, 'Capital and Cybernetics', 25, 25–28;

4   Ström, 'Capital and Cybernetics', 32.

5   Sam Meacham, 'A Race to Extinction: How Great Power Competition Is Making Artificial Intelligence Existentially Dangerous', *Harvard International Review*, 8 Sept 2023: hir. harvard.edu/a-race-to-extinction-how-great-power-competition-is-making-artificial-intelligence-existentially-dangerous/; Sven Lütticken, 'Shattered Matter, Transformed Forms: Notes on Nuclear Aesthetics, Part 1', *e-flux* 94, Oct 2018, 37–45: 39.

6   John Beck and Ryan Bishop, 'Introduction', eds. Beck and Bishop, *Cold War Legacies: Systems, Theories, Aesthetics* (Edinburgh: EUP, 2016), 1–32: 5.

7   Beck and Bishop, 'Introduction' to Beck and Bishop, *Cold War*

Eisenhower's military-industrial complex has expanded to become the military-industrial-university-entertainment complex that shapes relations among nations, corporations, educational institutions, entertainment industries and environmental policy, as well as structuring domestic and foreign policy in the US most notably — the various 'wars' conducted against abstractions such as 'drugs' or 'terror' — but also in Europe and beyond.[8]

As Tanizaki Jun'ichirō had realised in his consideration of the new consumerist Tokyo, the universal solvent for the military-industrial-university-entertainment complex is light. A flooding by light forces everything to open up to be known; it standardises space for evaluation and exchange, and is anchored by the transcendental authority of the light weapon. Universal light as a framework for evaluation, the basis of the nuclear regime as an arrangement of information, inevitably settles on the mediating technology of the screen — individuating, immobilising, virtuously reducing all to data. Paul Virilio makes this link explicit in *War and Cinema* — nuclear deterrence normalises surveillance as a public good, recreating the social realm as one 'based upon ubiquitous orbital vision of enemy territory'.[9]

The nuclear deterrent has always welcomed the screen as the apotheosis of the abstraction of conflict. The creation of SAGE (Semi-Automatic Ground Environment) networking systems, which have been co-ordinating Atlantic detection and response since the late '50s, meant that nuclear command was based entirely in a screen-mediated set of signals, effectively overriding sensory information and suggesting

---

Legacies, 12.

8   Beck and Bishop, 'Introduction' to Beck and Bishop *Cold War Legacies*, 10.

9   Virilio, *War and Cinema*, 2.

problems for our faith in empiricism.[10] The enthusiastic acceptance of Trident by positive-feedback Thatcherites from 1979 was followed by an explosive growth of public surveillance, trialled during Thatcher's second and third governments; within a couple of decades the UK would become a world leader in population tracking. Growing under both Thatcher and Blair administrations, mass surveillance is a Lockean social good: public space, in order to be public, has to keep yielding up data with value that can be exchanged, since property was a condition of social belonging. Privacy, like disarmament, is in this sense profoundly unpatriotic. The imperative to cut labour costs, moreover, forces mediated communication online, where it is increasingly subject to evaluation. Eventually, moving into the light of the screen (social media, form-filling, 'meetings') becomes a condition of belonging, even of survival.

If the toxic tendencies of the unifying light were beginning to come under criticism after the millennium, the universal screen would nevertheless be given a new moral imperative by the Covid lockdowns of 2020–21, at the gateway to the third nuclear era. The couple of years covering the lockdowns offered great opportunities for space control. Google's value more or less doubled; a new round of nuclear arming went largely unreported; and 'sheltering in place' in front of the world-filtering screen became compulsory. As Franco Berardi points out, lockdowns were not the origin of 'social distancing' — social distancing had long been a requirement of semiocapital — but lockdowns more or less turned the algorithmic isolation of the individual into a condition of citizenship.[11] In British 'public' institutions,

---

10   Beck and Bishop, 'Introduction' to Beck and Bishop *Cold War Legacies*, 17–18.

11   Franco Berardi, *Quit Everything: Interpreting Depression* (London: Repeater, 2024).

the term *meeting* came to mean the reduction of bodies to data to be sifted by Silicon Valley. Zoom meetings, like time and motion management, filter out irrational body movement, stripping away analogue signals to leave the person fully mediated, fully deterred.

The imperative of identity-value was particularly useful in crushing the political concerns of the class Dan Evans has called the petty-bourgeoisie — the class that once provided the duffel-coated earnest graduates of early CND.[12] Emotionally invested in their education but struggling with decreasing social mobility, the petty-bourgeoisie are forced to compete for cultural capital through identity and empathy performance, effectively becoming cultural enforcers and contributing to an algorithmic siloing that helps keep nuclear violence way beyond the imagination. In the American-led culture wars intensifying in the 2010s, fought between identities arrayed before screens, the nuclear violence threatening the cold dark millennia became virtually invisible. Nuclear realism benefits when the lower-middle class are squeezed and have to find the means of survival in short-term issues. This disciplining of the enforcing class is not that surprising. Nuclear weapons authority is one of the purest expressions of class power there is, forcing populations to embrace their role as the already bartered, the digitised and pre-sold. Evans's petty-bourgeoisie, lifted out of solidarity but lacking access to the comfort of the real middle class, find it difficult to form class alliances, and become a vanguard in reducing conflict to identity-evaluation. The turn from nuclear issues to identity issues is maintained by this class, themselves invested in the education system with the highest university tuition fees in Europe, and ultimately beholden to the

---

12   Dan Evans, *A Nation of Shopkeepers: The Unstoppable Rise of the Petty-Bourgeoisie* (London: Repeater, 2023).

jargon of the nuclear hegemon with the highest university tuition fees in the world.

If the moral rationale of the world of evaluation is ultimately anchored in classical empiricist imperatives, the universality of screen mediation now suggests that 'empiricist government' might be slipping its leash, outgrowing any direct perception of the world. This sifting of the world might be described as a digitisation, a reduction to discrete values (and a reduction with a moral basis for progress-making that goes as far back as the imperial tail of the Scottish Enlightenment).[13] Universal digital mediation is the end of the Newtonian promise: truth is always curated by capitalist concerns and recast as many individual truths, making consensus impossible and completing Scarry's 'cancellation of the population'. The algorithmic silo, like the nuclear silo, gives rise to post-truth and a moral competition that is purely rhetorical, without ground or conclusion. Meanwhile, despite the promise of clarity in digital values, political powers still need nuclear information to exist in a space *apart from* ones and zeroes, relying on policies of ambiguity. Jean Baudrillard described this nuclear passage into the society of the simulation, emptying out what we used to think of as the political. As William Chaloupka glosses this, 'Nuclear opponents implicitly admit that nuclear war is a representation, then put that image in a rhetorical context that evolves (represents) the most profound absence possible... [creating a] new, negative totality on which to base political action'.[14] Nuclear battles and identity battles simultaneously compete to command

---

13   There is one example of this — influential in commercial empire — in the 'conjectural history' of the Adam Smith scholar Dugald Stewart, in which experience is reduced to median points that can be plotted in singular stories.

14   Chaloupka, *Knowing Nukes*, 8.

public truth, their claims 'circulated and... exchanged between the nuclear protagonists exactly like international capital'.[15]

For Baudrillard, then, nuclear threats are *the* gateway to post-truth, to the absorption of social stakes into the unifying light of the screen, and wars that can no longer be merely physical — for which critique of liberal assumptions he was duly chastised by American progressive intellectuals speaking from the world's most expensive universities.[16] Baudrillard argues that a lingering desire to see nukes as a decision made by the population just demonstrates a 'nostalgia for the real' — the nuclear condition has already marked the shift whereby official politics came to be understood as the competition of individual truths and identities ('playing the game of difference'). Permanent nuclear deterrence demands a 'planetary... annihilation of stakes', or Scarry's fully dephysicalised pseudo-fighting.[17] It demands constant gaslighting as a way of life, a compulsory belief in avowedly fictional languages, with all its old truisms — that nukes show strength and relevance to allies; that deterrence has been proven to work; that the arsenal reflects the will of the people and will only last as long as the present crisis; that it can't be un-invented. The nuclear war is only ever a war for perception management while waiting for the inevitable accident.

The screen, then, acts as a proxy for the space-unifying weapon. It dissolves the analogue bonds between people and things, and reveals all as data. This is the insistence on revelation Byung-Chul Han has described as pornocracy.[18]

---

15   Baudrillard, *Simulations* (New York: Semiotext[e], 1983), 60, 61.

16   Dir. and wr. Adam Curtis, *HyperNormalisation*, BBC, 2016.

17   Jean Baudrillard, trans. Paul Foss, Paul Patton, and Philip Beitchman, *Simulations* (New York: Semiotext[e], 1983), 58, 59–60.

18   Byung-Chul Han, trans. Erik Butler, *The Transparency Society*

This term, pornocracy, has its roots in the medieval era, but has had extinction implications since around the start of the twentieth century — Thomas Moynihan documents the Russian cosmist Nikolai Federov's association of the term with an overwhelming of the hormonal regulation needed for survival.[19] Pornocracy doesn't just mean the proliferation of images of dead-eyed sex (though it means this as well, and it's telling that in 2020, Pornhub, a concern with a history of hosting videos of sexual assault, took advantage of virtuous social distancing by offering free subscriptions, an initiative enthusiastically reported by American liberals).[20] Pornocracy is more than this; it is fundamentally a capture by revelation, a separation of the person from a world that can be fully commanded through the screen, and a removal from politics as an embodied project of future-creation, or even survival. Pornocratic power follows the space-unifying superweapon. So as American infotech assumed near-global reach over the post–Cold War era, it also promised infinite access to the world while algorithmically narrowing the world to the needs of American progressivism itself (Anthony Burgess's 'Propaganda. Subliminal penetration'). Pornocracy brings a great narrowing of desire and an apocalyptic threat in the form of the eclipse of attention — or the collapse of the political into the news cycle. This is the old collapse of the social to market exchange, taking the population down with it.

(Stanford, CA: Stanford University Press, 2015 (2012)).

19   Thomas Moynihan, *X-Risk: How Humanity Discovered its Own Extinction* (Falmouth: Urbanomic, 2020), 320.

20   Natasha Turak, 'Pornhub is offering free premium memberships to countries on coronavirus lockdown, sees traffic leap', CNBC, 20 March 2020: cnbc.com/2020/03/20/coronavirus-lockdown-pornhub-is-offering-free-premium-memberships.html

Thus the pairing of algorithmic siloing and nuclear re-arming, culture wars and extinction unconscious. As the Bulletin of Atomic Scientists' Doomsday Clock broke two minutes at the beginning of the 2020s, the culture wars reached a kind of crescendo, with the entertainment of woke versus anti-woke occupying a vast chunk of public attention. By the time of 'lockdown rearming', progressive politics seemed to have undergone complete capture by automation. The old meme of 'current year' captured this — claims for absolutely new politics are in fact absolutely predictable steps in a predetermined historicism, foreclosing change. The promise of newness, then, only seems to yield more stringent versions of the same. It is unsurprising that this moment also sees the breakthrough of AI tools that extend cognitive mapping, as well as ChatGPT's implicit attempt to freeze all ethics relative to the current profit needs of America in 2022. Like nuclear standoff, ChatGPT aims to end history. As Han points out, AI has no present it can only filter and re-present the material of the past, and its widespread use is an admission of the closure of the open future by the nuclear hegemon.

Tools like ChatGPT express the extinction unconscious that has been built under the nuclear Pax Americana in a number of ways besides the obvious. One briefly memed experiment involved asking ChatGPT about the morality of using a currently unacceptable term, out of earshot of anyone, in order to stop a global nuclear war. While it's probably not true that ChatGPT's answers tended towards nuclear apocalypse in order to avoid the unheard slur, it does see the two alternatives as roughly comparable; for me it described the question as a 'trolley-car problem', a puzzle involving two outcomes so unpalatable that it's too terrible to decide on either. That these are more or less moral equivalents suggests something dark about the expendability of populations unable to stick to a progressive line. Behind this can be seen the whole litany of 2010s American woke culture, the determination to rearrange populations for maximum value, overwriting actual collectives as contravening typological imperatives, effectively arithmeticising populations. Genocidal corporate objectives were readily overlaid on top of progressive politics at the zenith of American woke capital, often becoming coterminous with it. Few were surprised when, in 2022–23, Lockheed Martin, the world's largest nuclear weapons manufacturer, drastically upped its investment in inclusion branding and made themselves highly visible at Pride marches. Meanwhile, since embodied connections are anathema to the identity-extinction complex, more and more forms of physical contact — forms that escape mediation by typology for profit — are seen as toxic, and are being overtaken by the Silicon Valley eugenics of algorithmic dating, ubiquitous porn, identitarian social media (all means of hijacking survival mechanisms). This is the great disarming that follows the spread of the identity-extinction complex.

Along with the fraying of American empire around the start of the 2020s, though, there was also an increased cultural registration of the way the mediating screen channels exterminism. The icon of the smartphone had by now taken on something like the role the mushroom cloud had played in the Cold War. Adam McKay's 2021 film *Don't Look Up*, typically seen as a parable on climate change, is more fundamentally a story of complicity in the narrowing of attention and the 'foreverist' avoidance of threats too overwhelming to think about — nicely imaged by the use of Xanax among the film's media professionals. What are the planetary threats standing just beyond the attention commanded by the screen? In the year the film was released alone, the US spent over \$42bn on nuclear weapons (and this was before the invasion of Ukraine).[21] In this film, a team of astronomers fail to generate interest in the world-ending threat, which is now too easy to relegate to the realm of the unthinkable. Media and politicians are unable to see beyond immediate digital imperatives, and the extinction event is always strangely inevitable. The extinction unconscious can be seen even in the opening scenes of the film, in the anomalous way PhD researcher Kate looks up into the skies rather than down at her smartphone, then fails to get Americans to act like the empiricists they used to be and still think they are.

There are other signs of extinction desire within ChatGPT itself. One briefly-memed experiment involved asking it about the morality of using a currently inappropriate term in order to stop a global nuclear war. The assertion that GPT tends to choose global nuclear war over the unheard personal slur was probably overstated; but for me it gave the question back as a 'trolley-car problem', a philosophical puzzle showing two outcomes so unpalatable that it's too terrible to decide on either. The fact that it is as easy to imagine the end of the world as to imagine a currently unfavoured term darkly signals the hold of American infotech over progressive politics at the end of a long period of nuclear hegemony. In fact, the culture wars were full of this kind of will to extinction, exacted as a price for universal individual affirmation. The briefly notorious 2019 Gillette ad 'We Believe', for example, perhaps representing one peak of late-'10s American woke, is really most remarkable for its pseudo-progressive desire to sift people into typologies to be virtuously removed. Here unmediated public encounters are blocked for reasons that can go unstated because they have been made so automatic (murky human

---

21   Congressional Budget Office, 'Projected Costs of US Nuclear Weapons, 2021–2030', 2021: cbo.gov/publication/57240

interactions are toxic, guilt is carried by race, and so on). The auto-progessive steps in, and the sexes are separated: she is sent back to the dating app's Silicon Valley eugenics, he to PornHub. Behind this is a dark erasure by typology — in the same way as in corporate and state versions of anti-racism, algorithmically-created groups are used to block out any spaces where people might have been able to collectivise. The point is not so much that 2010s American woke crowded out other issues, but that it enabled a great depoliticisation in line with the apocalyptic threat of the great nuclear weapons power. Embodied connections, this kind of culture shows, are anathema to the identity-extinction complex. Rather than well-meaning missteps forced by the culture wars, it suggests a pinnacle of the extinction unconscious, in which the progressive comes to coincide with a grim hyper-capitalism that expects to take over survival systems. Few were surprised when, in 2022–23, Lockheed Martin, the world's largest nuclear weapons manufacturer, drastically upped its investment in inclusion branding and made themselves highly visible at Pride marches.[22]

As it happens, nuclear arsenals' role in nihilistic individualism's occupation of solidarity was a relatively common cultural trope in the late Cold War. In Alasdair Gray's *Lanark* (1981), the protagonist's disease, hardening his skin and separating him from the rest of the world, is likened to nations' developing the armour of nuclear threat.[23] In a 1984 nuclear-themed number of the literary journal *Diacritics* (now best remembered for the contribution of Jacques Derrida), Frances Ferguson describes how 'that which is

---

22   Mint Press, 'Lockheed Martin took part in Pride Month', 2023: youtube.com/watch?v=WdDytTfT2kQ

23   Alasdair Gray, *Lanark* (Edinburgh: Canongate, 1981).

destroyed by [nuclear] self-destruction is exactly the self as the transcendental subject' — which is to say that through nukes, the empiricist self that can reduce the world to evaluation inevitably comes to enact its own annihilation.[24] The dream of a singular empiricist process, no longer able to adapt, and giving in to market determinism, inevitably collapses into a lonely confusion. By the time of this nuclear bonfire of subjectivity, the self has become inextricable from the economically rational reduction of the self to identity, and has come to embrace its own extinction. There are economic rewards for producing platforms that save labour costs by gluing users to compulsory platforms that make communication more difficult and cast the evisceration of contact as a strange social good by eviscerating human contact — the algorithm as extinction-worship, as a means of the nuclear condition.

So also the identity-extinction complex, working in the liberal tradition of abstracting violence (the 'disarming' of Jacobites that solidifies the British union), seeks to define violence as whatever interrupts evaluation; and as we know from Hiroshima and the IEA, since those who disturb the stability of evaluation are not really human, so limitless violence can and should be leveraged against them. Those interrupting the extraction of value as identity during the culture wars could be cancelled, and their cancellation would have a desirable chilling effect, make collective determination difficult, help cut labour costs, and help keep an anxious petty-bourgeoisie in line before they start to get any ideas about macro-violence. If this was neoliberal disciplining disguised as progress, it was also part of the wider removal of political stakes described by Elaine Scarry. How might a revival of physical stakes look? It would likely look

---

24   Frances Ferguson, 'The Nuclear Sublime', *Diacritics* 14–2, Summer 1984, 4–10.

toxic, in the way that the ritual suicides following the death of Emperor Meiji era looked toxic, and eventually marked illiberal Japan as an atomic target. Re-embodiment would likely involve a revival of memory and attention. It would also likely involve a rejection of algorithmic mediation by dissident collectives. And as Pelopidas has stressed, any avoidance of progressive extinction would depend on cultures making the real, immanent violence thinkable.

NUCLEAR WAR
AS THINKABLE

According to many nuclear commentators, populations don't make decisions about the exterminist weapon so much as the exterminist weapon makes decisions about them. Biological actors are liabilities in nuclear command chains, left, in a real emergency, trying to make extinction-level decisions while struggling with their own hormonal reactions and the ruins of deterrence logic. Nuclear decisions gradually remove themselves from human interference via the degree of obfuscation and ambivalence needed by the security state, and via the huge delays built into the declassification of sensitive documents — routinely twenty-five years or more — so that the conditions surrounding crises can never feed into any ongoing conversation. As Scarry points out about the fuzziness of communication with deep nuclear subs, a race for speed and clarity also involves an increase in slowness and confusion. Nuclear decisions are where any circulation of information necessary to democracy breaks down; and the Cold War and the period after are full of signs of terminal communicative failure.

By now there's a fair cultural memory of a few of these incidents, particularly the 1983 episode involving Stanislav Petrov (*The Man Who Saved the World*, as he was described in the title of the 2014 docudrama, which cast Kevin Costner next to Petrov himself). Petrov was a Soviet missile operator who disobeyed official protocol that expected him to facilitate launch, one of the most important events of the late twentieth century. But to the Petrov Save could be added many other incidents, some declassified, some lost, many failing to break through the algorithmic permafrost and forming an unseen trail left behind us on the path to the certain accident. By 2014, thirteen incidents had been logged between 1962 and 2002 when the world approached all-out nuclear war — all of them under conditions of less risk (according to Doomsday-Clock measurements) than in the 2020s.[1] As well as the hundreds of identifiable points of low-level dysfunction in hair-trigger military command systems, instances of clumsiness at the top have also been fairly common, though their stories are often little known. In 1979, President Carter sent the nuclear biscuit containing secret launch codes to a dry cleaner's.[2] In 1995, Russian Premier Boris Yeltsin, struggling with alcohol problems, had the nuclear launch device readied for a strike on the US because of the trace of a Norwegian scientific research rocket.[3] Bill Clinton's staff lost the nuclear codes for weeks and covered it up. From 2021 to 2024, the Democratic Party machinery disguised the cognitive incapability of the president while castigating Putin as nuclear madman; and the best replacement found for this was an unstable post-truth narcissist.[4]

---

1   Patricia Lewis, Heather Williams, Benoît Pelopidas and Sasan Aghlani, *Too Close for Comfort: Cases of Near Nuclear Use and Options for Policy* (Washington DC: Brookings University Press, 2014); Eric Schlosser, *Command and Control* (London: Penguin, 2013).

2   Atomic Heritage Foundation, 'Nuclear Briefcases', 12 June 2018: https://ahf.nuclearmuseum.org/ahf/history/nuclear-briefcases/.

3   Scarry, *Thermonuclear Monarchies*, 54.

4   Annie Linksey, 'How the White House Functioned with a Diminished Biden in Charge', *Wall Street Journal*, 19 Dec 2024:

But as tempting as it is to ascribe post-2024 risk to Trumpian volatility, Trump inherited an already complex set of hybrid wars and threats. The 2019 BBC series *Years and Years* has Trump launch a nuclear attack on a Chinese island, a familiar enough moment of instability, though with no real consequences in a largely incoherent story.[5] But this also raises the question of the attachement to nuclear threat in upper government building over decades before Trump. The demands of the culture wars made it difficult to imagine nuclear aggression by a Democrat president. But the only use of nuclear weapons on populations in history was ordered by a Democrat: President Truman. Under Kennedy, the Democrats established the policy of overkill, or overarming beyond the needs of the destruction of populations, and helped make the nuclear military-industrial complex unassailable, while Stuart Hall and other New Left proponents of non-alignment were citing the Republican Eisenhower's concerns over how this complex eclipsed populations. And like it or not, the only president to decisively move on nuclear disarmament was Ronald Reagan. Nuclear thinkability requires a detachment from the culture war dualities that have drafted in Europeans to focus on rivalries in the imperial centre. The road to nuclear thinkability lies more in thinking about a wider collapse of the singular progress that had demanded space-unifying weapons in the first place. Nuclear thinkability may now be rising with the erosion from American hegemony, as the Disney-Columbia axis of influence fades and new choices about non-alignment appear. In any case, nuclear violence does have to be thinkable, and there is always a danger in

---

wsj.com/politics/biden-white-house-age-function-diminished-3906a839

5   Wr. Russell T. Davies, dir. Simon Cellan Jones and Lisa Mulcahy, *Years and Years* (BBC, 2019).

letting this fall into retro or Fisher's (Frederic Jameson's) 'nostalgia mode'. Failing to register nuclear violence in an embodied present means an effective hardwiring of the extinction that is waiting for the certain accident or the angry president. This is the problem with *Threads* nostalgia: it turns one of the most political calls to thinkability into a comforting horror reflex, offering what Bertholt Brecht described as a catharsis, a way of finding relief and quietening political questions.[6]

Again, the Kyoto School could have helped with this negotiation with nihilism, had they not been marked down as an enemy after their own nuclear disciplining. Nuclear cultures engage in a tricky dance with absence. They have to deal with a particularly intransigent version of what often used to be called the Anthropocene — the irreversible modification of the environment pointing towards a disorienting world after humans. The nuclear condition shows that the Anthropocene was anchored by the assumption that the command of space was a foundation of progress. Timothy Morton describes how the 'end of the world' dates back to the condition following from James Watt's steam engine; but Watt was a product of the Scottish Enlightenment that followed the Newtonian-Lockean imperative to makes all places evaluable and useful. A deterministic progress kicks in; there is a disavowal of both pollution on geological timescales and — less spectacularly — the inevitable accident of the nuclear arsenal. This is the nuclear unconscious as a civilizational limit point, as something seemingly impossible to avoid and increasingly difficult to

---

6   Pelopidas, 'Imaginer la possibilité de la guerre nucléaire pour y faire face', 22; for Drew Milne the unthinkability of nuclear conflict has at times been idealised even by nuclear critics: 'Poetry After Hiroshima', 87, 92, 94; Ele Carpenter, *The Nuclear Culture Sourcebook* (London: Black Dog, 2016).

register as a political problem. If the 'end of the world' as a process of objectification originated in the eighteenth century, its terminal over-extension, its civilisational Autumn, is seen in the nuclear weapon. The hardwiring of the nuclear weapon is where liberal ideals run out of space, showing themselves unable to maintain the conditions for life.

There is something telling in the way the Climate Anthropocene now really has any traction in public debate, since it is the nuclear Anthropocene that embodies the very condition of forgetting the Anthropocene needs. By implication at least, the Climate Anthropocene is reachable by medium-term actions; its progress is non-inevitable. The Nuclear Anthropocene has less temporal accessibility — it is both unthinkably long and disorientingly immediate. The Climate Anthropocene presents itself as prosperity, so it seems open to arguments around economic growth. The Nuclear Anthropocene presents itself as security, as an existential necessity. The Climate Anthropocene has institutional purchase, while the perpetual absence of the Nuclear Anthopocene makes it pointless as institutional currency. Both mark the 'end of the world'; both look something like the destiny of the liberal subject, whose stability comes at the cost of the world created for it.

For some nuclear commentators or artists, though, the artificial radionuclide is the outstanding example of a human creation that denies humans a vantage point from which to see it. The condition of nuclear standoff, for Baudrillard, signals the end of critical distance, crushing a politics of representation, and burying morality under spectacle. In this sense, the desire for a history outside of the time of nuclear weapons is a desire for a public morality no longer open to this civilizational timeline. Or the artificial radionuclide is the doom of Atlantic progress, because it is the object that will not stay an object. The radionuclide hyperobject ushers in strange presences that settle over the biological as a will to extinction only recognised beyond the acceptable bounds of meaning — the building insanity of Ronald Craven, who in Kennedy Martin's *Edge of Darkness* is led by his dead daughter Emma to see the world after humans as we know them have gone. This hyperobject is what eludes the empiricist gaze, and its representation always tends to post-truth. In Peter Sloterdijk's provocative argument, the nuclear weapon slips out of visibility to become a kind of Buddha, forcing us to overcome violent ambitions.[7] In Jaime Semprun's post-Situationist parody *The Nuclearisation of the World* (1980), the nuclear channeling of 'the boundless social power constituted by the existence of market relations' allows the bomb to become its own ecology, acting 'on the very structure of inorganic matter... [so that] from now on there is no longer anything to see'.[8]

If the Nuclear Anthropocene has been relatively under-considered by environmentalists, still it weighs heavily in some twenty-first century nuclear artwork — work surrounding the Nuclear Culture Research Project, for example, which often speculates about ways to suggest the massive timescales involved.[9] In general, the Nuclear Anthropocene remains a victim of its own unthinkability, and the burdens of the terrible immediacy involved. The Nuclear Anthropocene is, as Tom Clancy's 1991 title

---

7   Peter Sloterdijk, trans. Michael Eldred, *Critique of Cynical Reason* (University of Minnesota Press, 1987 (1983)), 130–1.

8   Jaime Semprun, *The Nuclearization of the World*, 1980: libcom. org/article/nuclearization-world-jaime-semprun.

9   Ele Carpenter, 'Fluid Encounters Between Art & Science', 2016: nuclear.artscatalyst.org/content/fluid-encounters-between-art-science

had it, 'the sum of all fears': it is the understanding of an immediate extinction *telos* baked into the progress itself.

In fact, the alteration of the biology-earth relationship inherent in the nuclear weapon was fundamental to the Anthropocene concept. For the Anthropocene Working Group, Paul J. Crutzen and others, an origin of the Anthropocene era was the New Mexico tests — undertaken while knowing the weapon's extinction-level implications, with the 'father of the Hydrogen Bomb' Edward Teller describing nuclear-triggered extinction as likely.[10] Nukes are the overarching marker of biological expulsion, existing beyond embodied history and standing for the impossibility of occupying embodied history. They point to the limit on all life marked by the imperative to control all space, an imperative upstream of any decisions on carbon. One of the great markers of the world without meaning, moreover, is fallout dust — organic and inorganic stuff swept up indiscriminately and given unnatural powers to eclipse human history. Nuclear material, as Adam Piette puts it,

> acts as a form of message sent to the aftermath of the apocalypse, an expressive object aimed towards the deep geological future. The capsules of waste speak forwards to a time when we are a vanished race, presenting as our far future sepulchres, our treasures and our fetters, sealed with the spectral blood of the species.[11]

10   Paul J. Crutzen and John W. Birks, 'The Atmosphere after a Nuclear War: Twilight at Noon', *Ambio* 11-2/3, 114–25; Peter C Van Wyck, 'The Anthropocene's Signature', in ed. Ele Carpenter, *The Nuclear Culture Sourcebook* (London: Black Dog, 2016), 23–30, 2016; Jan Zalasiewicz et al., 'When Did the Anthropocene Begin? A Mid-Twentieth Century Boundary Level Is Stratigraphically Optimal', *Quaternary International* 383 (2015), 196–203.

11   Adam Piette, 'Between Geological Disposal and Radioactive

The question of how to depict such a total and ever-haunting absence is as old as the nuclear age itself. The 1945 bombings ushered in a great wave of consideration of extinction as the fate of all species. One early vehicle for the unimaginable was alien anthropo-archaeology: the viewpoint of extraterrestrial visitors wondering about human self-destruction. In *Sometime Never* (1948), Roald 'Chocolate Factory' Dahl has alien visitors watching the chaos of self-destructive world wars till they feel they have to take over.[12] In Pelham Groom's *The Purple Twilight* (1948), Earth settlers on Mars try to explain the Terran nuclear ambitions that had ended in 'all the cities in England being smitten with Atomic bombs'.[13] Leo Szilard, nuclear visionary then anti-nuclear campaigner, himself turned to alien anthropology fiction. In one story his extraterrestrials speculate that human extinction had had something to do with coins, which at first they think are toilet tokens, but come to understand as money — something 'subject to great fluctuations vaguely reminiscent of the manic-depressive cycles of the insane... [making] a depressive-phase war... possible even within the same species'.[14]

However, if the Anthropocene fate of nuclear-armed civilisations found a home in the alien anthropology, this kind of creative considerations of species' lifespans would

Time: Beckett, Bowen, Nirex and Onkalo', in eds. Beck and Bishop, *Cold War Legacies*, 102–15: 113.

12   Roald Dahl, *Some Time Never: A Fable for Supermen* (London: Collins, 1948).

13   Pelham Groom, *The Purple Twilight* (London: T. Werner Laurie, 1948).

14   Leo Szilard, 'Report on "Grand Central Terminal', *The Voice of the Dolphins and Other Stories* (London: Victor Gollancz, 1961 (1948)).

soon fade.[15] This probably signaled some wearied acceptance of the nuclear condition, but the effects of astrobiol-
ogy and alien-watching also registered, as in SETI's (Search
for Extraterrestrial Intelligence) suggesting lower-than-ex-
pected chances for the spontaneous development of life,
thus making the self-destructive condition truly omnicidal.
Szilard's collaborator on the first nuclear pile, Enrico Fermi,
is now best known for the Fermi Paradox, which asks why,
although calculations show that extraterrestrial life should
exist, increasingly powerful searches show no signs. This
condition of 'cosmic loneliness' is the final issue of thinkability — the question of an absence that already hangs
over the present and structures it in a way that can only
be hinted at and never fully described, leaving no ground
for meaning, memory or narrative. But this omnicide is the
telos of the singular progress that turns the world to value,
eventually replacing biological weakness with money form
designed to outlast them — Szilard's toilet tokens.

In which case, the object of the imagination on a path
marked by extinction-level weapons is a radical absence.
The real measure of the terminal commitment to extinction-level weapons is not the deaths of national populations, as such dangers are often imagined ('an attack could
devastate the UK'); nor is it the death of all human life, like
the edgier Climate Anthropocene writers might imagine
('it's time to leave the ruins to other species'); nor is it even
the end of all life on earth. The thinkability struggle, as
well as the struggle to have the extinction-bound arms race
seen as political, is also the struggle over the fate of biological life. People don't decide whether or not to embrace the
extinction unconscious; omnicide is always there, nullify-
ing all intention, gradually robbing the political of mean-

---

15   Though Martin Amis has a retro pop at the sub-genre in his
Einstein's Monsters (1987).

ing. In which sense, thinking nuclear war is, in a strange way, thinking the conditions of a life that can still be lived. The physical effects of apocalypse, the short torture and the cold dark millennia, but also the possible languages of disarmament communications, all mark a belief that a universe of life is possible.

To some degree this thinkability is racing against real collapse, and the embrace of the inevitable accident. Cognitive dissonance is much in evidence here, as the post-war nuclear club of world-leading nations struggle to give up their addictions. If Tony Blair thought that disarmament 'risk[ed] too much of a downgrading of our status as a nation', surely now another risk for the UK is that it comes to be seen as basketcase nuclear tyranny. The British press put nuclear weapons states like Russia and North Korea on constant collapse-watch, while the UK itself seems to have no minimum level of social and political functioning beneath which a nuclear arsenal is morally unjustifiable. We see this in the credibility of public communication, the lifeblood of democracy as someone like Elaine Scarry would understand it. We see it in railway departure boards — in twenty-first-century Britain, a site of auto-generating post-truth messages that are still habitually seen as a shared reference. The board's trains are 'expected' at specific times that passengers know not to have touched the expectation of any biological being at all — often that have already passed. There is no way of really registering this as untruth, with all staff who haven't already been downsized themselves dependent on the auto-generated information. The problem isn't that trains are not on time; it's that experienced truths so commonly fall under the threshold of thinkability, and leave no present for humans to determine. In such public spaces, non-biological prostheses of emotion abound: expectation (the train time), anticipation ('Get excited!'), regret ('We are sorry that...').

And crucially the registering of any resistance to the winding down of human intention is itself increasingly marked as toxic. Familiar NHS answer messages remind would-be patients that angry reactions to their emtrapment can cost them their 'healthcare'.[16] To function as citizen, you have to keep disavowing the violence. Passed through layers of (cybernetic/nuclear) abstraction, violence becomes plausibly deniable, and no-one is responsible for it — helping to explain the meteoric rise of the word 'unfortunately'. At heart, this disavowal is the disavowal of world-ending powers that operate just under the level of consciousness. Nuclear weapons are unfortunate weapons.

This slide of public communications is described by CND veteran Doris Lessing in her 1974 novel *Memoirs of a Survivor*. Here, an agonisingly slow collapse is impossible to grasp in any given moment; it always seems to have happened before it can be notices, and the protagonist is left to undergo ritual daily walks to try to gather properly empirical, or unmediated, news. Trying to piece together the collapse, she reflects that 'for all of us there were moments when *the game we were all agreeing to play* simply could not stand up to events: we would be gripped by feelings of unreality, like nausea'.[17] The nausea always seems distant from the present. It is always anomalous, always unfortunate, and it will soon be overturned in some way no-one can yet imagine. But it really belongs to Pelopidas's disconnected future, and it is the permanent crisis enabled by nuclear abstraction.

Paradoxically, the more a nuclear deterrence mentality ravages political action, the more it is presented as a necessary source of security in a world of decreasing stability.

---

16   David Graeber picks up the situation of this NHS warning in *Bullshit Jobs* (London: Penguin, 2018).

17   Doris Lessing, *Memoirs of a Survivor* (London: Flamingo, 1995 (1974)), 20.

James Callaghan's Trident acquisition at Gaudeloupe took advantage of this, and E.P. Thompson diagnosed this situation, in which a perpetual threat of total violence can make sense in the formal economy while terminally driving down living standards and democratic participation and benefitting no-one.[18] This exhausting march of dissonance can go on for decades. Its combination of dysfunctionality, sociopathy and violence-acceleration is Orwellian in the serious sense. And in fact there's a nice example of the dissonant train as evisceration of the public in Michael Radford's 1984 film of *Nineteen Eighty-Four*, when John Hurt's Winston stares into a grimy carriage in ancient, battered rolling stock and braces himself under the official cheerfulness of the Spies. Or in *Children of Men*, as a filthy wire-meshed overground tube takes Theo into Zone 2, past burning garbage piles, security fences, stone-throwing gangs, caged refugees, and taped-over broken machines, with passengers trying to avoid the looping ads for suicide pills and UK exceptionalism — 'Only Britain soldiers on'. These are both post-nuclear stories, and they both explore the combination of totalising violence and performative care: the public as habit rather than belonging. The chirpy repeating ads in *Children of Men* offer palliative care to citizens who have long since given up — much like in Ray Bradbury's 1950 nuclear apocalypse short story 'There Will Come Soft Rains', in which a smart house keeps functioning for disappeared humans.[19] Nukes are the 'security' thriving as the substrate of this chaos. It's tempting to ask what British operatives would do — or what they *do* do — when faced with Petrov-type nuclear emergencies. Conceivably, they would treat real, incoming missiles much as we treat car

---

18   Thompson, 'Notes on Exterminism', 24.

19   Ray Bradbury, 'There Will Come Soft Rains', *Collier's*, 4 August 1950: miseroprospero.com/will-come-soft-rains/

alarms.[20] However the inevitable accident comes, it will be unfortunate.

The British thinkability crisis may be even worse than Petrov's situation. Petrov, like all Soviet citizens of the 1970s–80s, understood that the empire was collapsing under its own contradictions. The need to cope with the confusion of official truths was factored into everyday life and gave rise to informal trust communities. The maddening contradictions of bureaucratic imperatives would even take on a nuclear shorthand — Chernobyl: the 1986 incident that spread radiation across Europe after decades of official miscommunication. But twenty-first-century Atlantic equivalents for the calling of this everyday dissidence remain sparse; and in the UK, speech laws may well overtake them. By the 2020s, the hypocrisies of the old British state complained about by Orwell had developed into a world-leading cognitive dissonance. And the country that took the H-bomb as its birthright, sliding into a performative morality incapable of asking really moral questions, comes to look like, as Thompson described Britain, 'a caricature of an exterminist formation'.[21]

In fact, so strong is the habitual pull of 'Only Britain soldiers on' morality that the nuclear arsenal can be made to look not only like neutral defence, but like an anti-colonial gesture. When foreign secretary David Lammy castigated Russia at the United Nations in September 2024 — beginning by making the Ukraine War about himself, perhaps puzzlingly to some delegates, but recognised by Brits used

---

20   Julie McDowall points out that there were numerous false air-raid sirens during the New Cold War, some with scarring effects, some ignored, as in the alarm of February 1984 in Coventry, when 'many people simply turned over in their beds and went back to sleep': *Attack Warning Red!*, 21.

21   Thompson, 'Notes on Exterminism', 23.

to seeing race as a marker of moral legitimacy — he described 'imperialism. I know it when I see it'.[22] Kremlin ambitions are definitely imperialist; but there's a weird disjunction in Lammy's joining this to the vigorous acceleration of an apocalyptic threat. RAF Lakenheath had recently readied to receive American nukes, New START had been abandoned, and one of Lammy's government's first moves was to reaffirm the US-UK Mutual Defence Agreement on an 'enduring basis'.[23] Yet nukes, wielded by a government

22   David Lammy, 'Statement to UN Security Council, Foreign, Commonwealth and Development Office', 24 Sept 2024: gov.uk/government/speeches/putins-invasion-of-ukraine-is-in-his-interest-alone-to-expand-his-mafia-state-into-a-mafia-empire-uk-statement-at-the-un-security-council

23   Dave Cullen, 'Extreme Circumstances: the UK's new nuclear warhead in context' (London: Nuclear Information Service, August 2022), 16, 28, 44: nuclearinfo.org/wp-content/uploads/2022/08/Extreme-Circumstances-print-version.pdf; Tim Street, Harry Spencer, and Shane Ward, 'The British government doesn't want to talk about its nuclear weapons. The British public does', *Bulletin of the Atomic Scientists*, 6 April 2023: thebulletin.org/2023/04/the-british-government-doesnt-want-to-talk-about-its-nuclear-weapons-the-british-public-does/?utm_source=Twitter&utm_medium=SocialMedia&utm_campaign=TwitterPost032023&utm_content=NuclearRisk_BritishPublic_04062023; Mills, 'Amendments to the UK-US Mutual Defence Agreement', 24; Richard Norton-Taylor, 'Starmer permanently ties UK nuclear arsenal to Washington', *Declassified UK*, 3 September 2024: declassifieduk.org/starmer-permanently-ties-uk-nuclear-arsenal-to-washington/; Claire Mills, 'Amendments to the UK-US Mutual Defence Agreement' (London: House of Commons, 2024): researchbriefings.files.parliament.uk/documents/CBP-10086/CBP-10086.pdf, 4; Shannon Bugos, 'Understanding the Dispute over the New START', Arms Control Association, April 2023: armscontrol.org/act/2023-

drawing its legitimacy from natural law, are not themselves imperialist. In the same year, former US national security advisor Robert C. O'Brien recommended a return to nuclear testing, one of the great markers of global imperialism and the willingness to abandon the world at the altar of superpower rivalry — and all this before the accelerated instability of Trump-Vance.[24] Russia is redrawing borders

---

04/news/understanding-dispute-over-new-start. The 12000 US troops stationed in the UK remain effectively extra-legal, protected by the Visiting Forces Act and the Status of Forces Agreement (SOFA): House of Commons Library, US Forces in the UK: legal agreements, 2015: researchbriefings.files.parliament.uk/documents/SN06808/SN06808.pdf; Hans M Kristensen, Matt Korda, Eliana Johns, and Mackenzie Knight, 'United Kingdom nuclear weapons, 2024', *Bulletin of the Atomic Scientists*, 12 November 2024: thebulletin.org/premium/2024-11/united-kingdom-nuclear-weapons-2024/; A/Political, 'The Racket: Matt Kennard and Jeremy Corbyn', 2024: youtube.com/watch?v=XbmcNI0My_0&t=1366s.

24   Robert C. O'Brien, 'The Return of Peace Through Strength', *Foreign Affairs*, 18 June 2024: foreignaffairs.com/united-states/return-peace-strength-trump-obrien; Jessica T. Mathews, 'A new nuclear arms race is beginning, it will be far more dangerous than the last one', Guardian, 14 November 2024: theguardian.com/world/2024/nov/14/nuclear-weapons-war-new-arms-race-russia-china-us. The damage caused by nuclear testing is hard to quantify, but for one model by Arjun Makhijani and Tilman Ruff, major tests by Nuclear Weapons States (France, the UK, the US, the Soviet Union, China, India, Pakistan) had caused almost a million deaths from cancer alone by 2000 — International Physicians for the Prevention of Nuclear War/Physicians for Social Responsibility, *The Devastating Consequences of Nuclear Testing: Effects of Nuclear Weapons Testing on Health and the Environment*, 2023: ippnw.org/wp-content/uploads/2024/01/IPPNW_Report_Nuclear_Tests_EN.pdf. A lowered nuclear taboo has also revived discussions of

'by force', Lammy says as he stands in front of the extermination weapons his government had been using to carve out spheres of influence for eighty years, in contravention of the Non-Proliferation Treaty of the United Nations to which Lammy was now speaking. Nuclear threat is gunboat diplomacy on an extinction level, but the old moral high ground of non-violence allowed the British foreign secretary to present it as some kind of decolonial strategy.

What appears with the third nuclear age, though, is the opportunity, or the imperative, to Make Nukes Thinkable Again. This is the cultural challenge of seeing nuclear arming as a leveraging of real violence against foreign and domestic populations. Slipping the American nuclear umbrella could signal a great reorination of the thinkable; the escape from perpetual extinction blackmail might be paved with unsubscriptions from Zoom and Netflix. A de-aligned Europe, or a de-unified UK, could trigger a revivified interest in the world, as something exceeding the progressive expectations of the Pax Americana.[25] Languages of disarmament might displace its monoglot tendencies. If nuclear

---

nuclear winter, the blocking out of sunlight through radioactive dust, causing maybe two billion deaths from a 'minor' regional conflict — Lili Xia et al., 'Global food insecurity and famine from reduced crop, marine fishery and livestock production due to climate disruption from nuclear war soot injection', *Nature Food*, 12 August 2022: nature.com/articles/s43016-022-00573-0; Matthias Dörries, 'The Politics of Atmospheric Sciences: "Nuclear Winter" and Global Climate Change', *Klima* 26-1, 2011, 198–223.

25 I've touched on something like this in stories set in a Scotland influenced by animism, Jacobitism, and organic computing. In one, an engaged couple meeting near Helensburgh realise that the last qualms of their families concern the terrible presence that had once haunted that area, acknowledge the haunting presence of the nuclear threat and move on.

threat has remained a niche interest, there are already in place powerful equivalents of the Cold War consciousness-raising organisations that informed *Threads* or *The War Game*, including Nuclear Information Service, ICAN, and Declassified UK. The challenge is not even to demand disarmament as much as it is to make the real, ongoing violence imaginable.

ACKNOWLEDGEMENTS

I would like to thank these people who have helped in various ways, knowingly or unknowingly, with the writing of this book, but who are not responsible for any of its arguments.

Claire Westall, Alex Niven, Tariq Goddard, Carl Neville, Chris de Veau, Anthony Barnett, Sian Long, Paulo de Medeiros, Jen Baker, Richard Moore, Elizabeth Frazer, Daniel Cordle, Robert Gardiner, Shannon Bugos, Tim Street, Jeremy Gilbert, Li Toma, Tom Gray, Joe Jackson, Kris Stoddart.

A LIFE LIVED REMOTELY:

BEING AND WORK IN THE DIGITAL AGE

by

SIOBHAN MCKEOWN

A Life Lived Remotely tells the story of the transition to the digital age through our relationship to work. Following the author's journey as she left her 9-to-5 for the world of freelancing and working remotely, it outlines and reflects on what it means to work from home, how it affects our daily lives and our relationships, and how it is tied in to the development of the internet and our increasingly digitised world.

Tackling larger questions like What happens when we take our lives online?; How are we being changed by immersion in the internet?; and How do we know the difference between work and life when one seems to blend into the other?, A Life Lived Remotely provides a moment's pause in a world of fast-paced communication, offering critical reflection on what it means to come of age along with the internet.

TAIPEI AT DAYBREAK

by

BRIAN HIOE

How far would you got to fight for what is right?

When a Taiwanese American activist calling himself Q.Q. goes abroad in search of his missing friends, he winds up in Taipei. 2014 is the year of the Sunflower Movement in Taiwan, and Q.Q. finds himself drawn into the anti-government protests, navigating both his internal conflicts and battles wit his activists as he tries to establish an online magazine, Daybreak, in order to report the scale of what is happening in Taiwan to the wider world.

Taking place against the backdrop of Occupy Wall Street in America, the anti-nuclear protests in Japan, and the student protests in Taiwan, *Taipei at Daybreak* is an Asian American coming-of-age novel exploring nihilism, love, art, power, and what drives people to put themselves on the frontlines of conflict.

Available from RepeaterBooks.com

Code: Damp

An Esoteric Guide to British Sitcoms

by

Sophie Sleigh-Johnson

Code: Damp is a sometimes-comedic field report that charts an esoteric code hidden within the twin poles of 1970s sitcoms *Rising Damp* and *The Fall and Rise of Reginald Perrin*. Outlining how past cultural patterns condensate and repeat through technology, time is shown to be a damp condensation seeping through the centuries and out onto the telly.

Merging the vast with the parochial, the occult with the comedic, *Code: Damp* tunes into the weird demands of damp as a time-traveling material at the intersections of comedy, myth and technology, taking all three as serious resources to better (dis)orient the ground we stand on.

HOW THE RAILWAYS WILL FIX THE FUTURE

REDISCOVERING THE ESSENTIAL BRILLIANCE OF THE IRON ROAD

by

GARETH DENNIS

The world's railways were almost entirely created by capital and empire for extraction and exploitation, so what right do they have to exist and how can they be harnessed for good? Railway engineer and writer Gareth Dennis builds a case not simply for railways as a common good, but argues that railways are a critical tool for humanity to survive and thrive.

Dennis takes us across the globe, from Virgin Hyperloop's abandoned test track in the Nevada desert to the overcrowded stations of the North of England, exploring how railways can shape and inform choices about our future, and in turn detailing how taking a long-term view can help shape transport for the better. With his deep knowledge of railways and his unique view of history and politics, he equips us with the tools to answer those imperative questions: what and who should our railways be for?

FLUID FUTURES

SCIENCE FICTION AND POTENTIALITY

by

STEVEN SHAVIRO

Fluid Futures is about how science fiction imagines an open future. Science fiction does not claim to predict what will actually happen in times to come. But it offers pictures of potential developments; it narrates the unfolding of possibilities for change that are already implicit, or incipient, in the present moment. As Rod Serling said, science fiction is "the improbable made possible."

Shaviro insists upon the aboutness of science fiction, as it depicts situations and ideas that are at once possible and difficult to grasp. The book then explores how the genre embraces fictionality and narrative, reconceives time, and projects images of possible worlds. The point of the book is not to give a theory of science fiction. Instead, it emphasizes the ways that science fiction texts themselves propose theories, leading readers to reconceive concepts that we have taken for granted.

LIKE LOCKDOWN NEVER HAPPENED

MUSIC AND CULTURE DURING COVID

by

JOY WHITE

During the COVID-19 pandemic, music listening increased as people used it to help to counter the psychological fallout of lockdown and reduce its effects of isolation, restriction and boredom. At the same time, concerts and other musical events moved online, and even when lockdown eased, social distancing meant that group musical and cultural events took on a different format.

An attempt to make sense of chronological and kairotic time in the early era of the pandemic, this book explores the way that Black joy and sonic Black geographies were key to the culture of this period, and how Black music and Black creative expression soundtracked and sustained us during the pandemic.

REPEATER BOOKS

is dedicated to the creation of a new reality. The landscape of twenty-first-century arts and letters is faded and inert, riven by fashionable cynicism, egotistical self-reference and a nostalgia for the recent past. Repeater intends to add its voice to those movements that wish to enter history and assert control over its currents, gathering together scattered and isolated voices with those who have already called for an escape from Capitalist Realism. Our desire is to publish in every sphere and genre, combining vigorous dissent and a pragmatic willingness to succeed where messianic abstraction and quiescent co-option have stalled: abstention is not an option: we are alive and we don't agree.